LEWES

Two Thousand Years of History

"You can see Lewes lying like a box of toys under a green amphitheatre of chalk hills. On the whole it is set down better than any town I have seen in England."
(William Morris)

LEWES

Two Thousand Years of History

Barbara Fleming

S.B. Publications

First published 1994 by Barbara Fleming
in association with S.B. Publications
c/o 19 Grove Road, Seaford, East Sussex BN25 1TP

Reprinted 1997

Reprinted 2000

© Copyright (text) Barbara Fleming 1994

© Copyright (photographs) Barbara Fleming 1994

ISBN 1 85770 062 7

Typeset and Printed by Adland Print Group
Unit 11, Bellingham Trading Estate, Franthorne Way, London SE6 3BX
Telephone: 020 8695 6262 Facsimile: 020 8695 6300

CONTENTS

Front cover: The Battle of Lewes (based on an old manuscript)
The Lewes Shield: The blue and gold chequers are the arms of the de Warenne family. The gold lion rampant on the red ground is from the arms of the Earl of Arundel, nephew to the last Earl de Warenne.
(Reproduced by kind permission of the Mayor of Lewes)

Back cover: Priory ruins in the Grange Gardens.

Title page: View from the War Memorial down School Hill to Cliffe Hill.

ACKNOWLEDGEMENTS

I have many people to thank for the writing and production of this book. For the initial encouragement, Bridget Chapman of the Sussex Archaeological Society and, from then on, my good friend Barbara Hamilton-Smith of the Oxted History Society.

I am grateful for the use of so many books and papers in the Lewes Public Library and in the Library of the Sussex Archaeological Society at Barbican House, Lewes. My grateful thanks are also due to Gem Savage and to Harry Precey who, by their artistry, brought to life my demands for the front and back covers of the book.

My special thanks to Len Davey, again a fellow member of the Sussex Archaeological Society, for his meticulous correcting of the entire manuscript, and to Phil Flowers, of the Cliffe Bookshop, Lewes, for his very helpful comments. Also to Jenny and David Sanders for the initial word-processing and corrections, and to Peter Sanders for his much appreciated railway information.

My sincere thanks too, to Mr Edward Reeves for reproducing the illustrations from my slides, and to Lee Simpson for Plate 13.

Lastly, publishing would not have been accomplished without the generous encouragement and help of David Arscott and Steve Benz, to whom I am especially grateful.

LIST OF MAPS

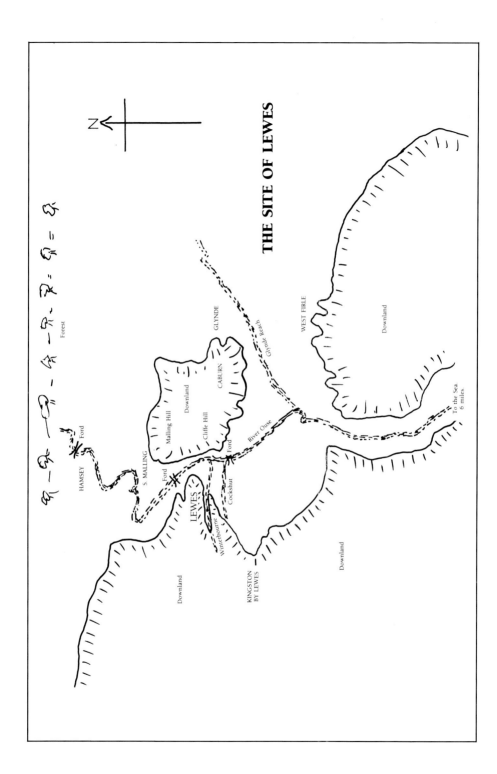

THE SITE OF LEWES

Forest

HAMSEY
Ford

S MALLING
Ford

Malling Hill

Downland

Cliffe Hill

CABURN

GLYNDE

Glynde Reach

Ford

River Ouse

LEWES

Cockshut

Winterbourne

KINGSTON
BY LEWES

Downland

Downland

WEST FIRLE

Downland

To the Sea
6 miles

N

INTRODUCTION

THE SITE OF LEWES

Lewes, despite its location only fifty miles from the Capital, nestles into the escarpment of the South Downs as one of the least known of all the county capitals of England. From the point of view of self-preservation this has not been such a disadvantage, public attention can change a town out of all recognition as it did her neighbour along the coast, Brighthelmstone.

It lies, enfolded in history, in the lovely downland landscape of South-east England. In fact it can claim to be as old as England is herself, since it was first founded, as a settlement, in Anglo-Saxon times and derives its name from the Saxon word for a hill, "hlaew".

That Lewes has been so little remarked throughout history, and indeed is still today, is primarily due to her geographical location, arising from the underlying geological structure of this corner of the British Isles. Here the strata stretch in bands parallel to the Channel Coast and act as a permanent barrier for over thirty miles inland.

Along the coast line itself rises the belt of chalk averaging eight miles wide and from four to five-hundred feet high, this is part of the South Downs. A narrow belt of fertile Greensand edges the northern scarp-slope of the Downs, scarcely the width of two small farms, and north of this again stretches the vast, flat expanse of the heavy clays of Wealden Sussex. Until the 16th century this was almost impenetrable indigenous forest for the traveller, oak and ash and thorn rooted in the ill-drained "clegg", too wet and sticky for passage in the winter and iron-rutted in the summer. Northward of this rises the sandstone ridge of the High Weald, again forested and unwelcome to the traveller of old, to be backed by a matching belt of Wealden clay similar to that to the south.

This huge barrier, thirty miles wide and a hundred and twenty miles long from east to west, the fearsome "Andredswald" of the Saxons, virtually walled off this corner of England. Isolated in this way, East Sussex developed strikingly independent characteristics. These were not stunted, since wide contacts by sea were maintained from the first with Europe and beyond, but the region could afford to be less subservient to the central authority of the realm in many aspects of its life and to direct its activities and its thinking into independent channels still traceable to this day.

Two rivers cut through this part of the Weald, rising in the Forest Ridge and draining through valleys in the chalk to the sea, the Sussex Ouse and the Cuckmere. Of these, the Ouse provides by far the most navigable waterway and, from earliest times, also provided a valuable port at its estuary, first at Seaford and later at Newhaven. Lewes lies on the Ouse eight miles inland from the sea. Here it was well protected from most of the sea-raiders of history and lay at a crucial point where the west to east ancient Downland trackway forded the river at a narrow constriction in the Ouse valley. Thus it was excellently placed as a centre for land-marketing and also for the coastal-shipping of all the mineral and agricultural wealth of the hinterland.

The town itself was first developed on a small spur of chalk which protrudes across the Ouse valley as a west-to-east finger of Downland from the northern escarpment. The High Street runs west to east along the backbone of the spur and dips over the nose of it straight down to the river at Cliffe. Now, building has spread over the valley on all sides, southwards over a second spur as Southover, northwards over the Downland foothills in three small estates and in a narrow band along the river, from Malling in the north, to Southerham in the south. Development here is limited to the line of the river by the rising outlier of chalk due east of the river comprising Mount Caburn, Malling Hill and Cliffe Hill.

A fine panoramic view of the site and setting of the town can be obtained from the top of the castle-keep behind the High Street. To the west the high land flattens out into Downland as far as the eye can see. Looking south down the Ouse valley, the land rolls wide and green, lined intermittently on each side of the valley, along the spring-line, with flint-built villages. To the south-east is the crest of Firle Beacon and nearer at hand the steep sides of Caburn Hill.

Lewes spur to the west, and Mount Caburn to the east, squeeze the Ouse valley into a width of some three hundred yards at its narrowest point. In early days a tributary of some importance, the Winterbourne, carved a waterway from the west around the south of the spur, to the River Ouse here. On this, in Medieval times, was the Watergate of the town, the road to this is still known as Watergate Street. But this is now hidden from the castle view-point, by housing and railway development. Neatly tamed and channelled it is now only a feature of the Grange Gardens of Southover.

Lastly, looking north-east from the town, the Low Weald still sweeps in unbroken flatness for mile after mile. It is no longer impenetrable forest, though there are still scattered woodlands. On the horizon, the High Weald, now the Ashdown Forest, completes the view.

I. THE EARLIEST YEARS

Prehistoric Lewes

The first evidence of any sort of settlement on the Lewes spur dates from the Roman occupation of the first century A.D. The River Ouse being a navigable waterway from the sea, it was one of the possible points of Roman invasion and, in the murky depths of the Weald, was the already established, primitive iron-industry to encourage further penetration.

The Downlands and their fertile greensand footings had already been settled and were farmed in a scattered, rural pattern. Caburn and Ranscombe Hill were surmounted by pre-Roman hill-forts and were fortified sites of considerable size which did not, however, survive the Roman Conquest. The ditches and mounds of these are still plainly visible today. The climb to the top of Mount Caburn, from Ringmer or from Glynde, is open to walkers and very rewarding. The bank and ditch formations are easily followed and the view from the summit, as from Lewes, is panoramic.

The other relics on the surface, of the Iron Age and earlier, are not so easily recognised. They consist of parallel embankments on the Downland slopes. These are the remains of primitive ploughing along the contours of the chalk hill. A row of houses along Malling Street below one example remembers them in its name, "The Lynchets".

Roman Lewes

The Romans marched into Britain in their disciplined legions between 43 and 49 A.D. Whether there was fighting in this area, particularly on Mount Caburn, is not recorded. They appreciated the value of the site of Lewes enough to establish a fort there to guard the river crossing and the narrow neck of land around it. No doubt the stronghold, now showing as a rectangular earthwork in the churchyard of the Church of St. John-sub-Castro, was part of the full defence system maintained by the Romans to guard the entire south-east coast of their British colony.

It is commemorated by a plaque on a small row of houses named after it, "The Fosse", along Lancaster Street. The fosse was a ditch surrounding the fort in which the houses are said to be built. It is well worth a turn into the churchyard, through the gate at the end of Church Row, to appreciate to the full what a strategic point this was. From here one can picture the solid river craft moving laboriously along the Ouse below and the wagons of grain or animal skins lurching along the Roman road that threaded the gap beside the river.

Pottery, coins and rings etc. of the Roman period have been unearthed locally. Traces of Roman villas as farm settlements are widespread along the coast of Sussex, particularly on the greensand soils. Also there is plenty of evidence of Roman road-making. But no Roman building has been unearthed in Lewes itself. The road from London has been conclusively traced across the Weald via

Edenbridge down as far as Malling Down. A branch turned westwards at Barcombe to run across the southern edge of the forest to East Chiltington, Streat and Ditchling. Eagle eyes can make out traces of the "aggers" alongside hedges on route. A house in the almost vanished hamlet of Chiltington claims its name of "The Romans" is based on the above road crossing its land. There are scattered relics of roads further north, across the Weald, and also east and west across the greensand area.

Interestingly enough, although they came originally from a city built on seven hills, when it came to establishing cities in its colonies, the Romans almost invariably chose sites that were flat. No doubt it made it easier to achieve their meticulously laid-out grid plan and to manoeuvre their horse-drawn traffic. True to type, when they pulled out of Britain three hundred years or so after they had arrived, they appear to have left no town on the spur to crumble into desolation like their villas on the plain below.

Doubtless the legionary heaved a sigh of relief at saying farewell to this remote island defence post threatened by hill, forest and sea in 410 A.D. One assumes the British natives may, initially, also have heaved a sigh of relief. No more taxes, no more forced labour and slavery . . . . Ominously it was only the calm before the storm and a great deal worse was to lie ahead.

Britain slid slowly into that twilight in history known as the Dark Ages.

The deserted cities and the elegant villas decayed and life took on the scattered, rustic look it had presented before the Roman Conquest. The south-east coastlands remained as vulnerable to attack as they had been in 49 A.D. and so the inevitable happened. In 477, as the Anglo-Saxon Chronicle so unemotionally states, "Aella came to Britain and his three sons, Cymen, Wlencing and Cyssa with three ships . . . . They killed many Welsh (their name for the British local inhabitants) and drove some in flight into the Weald."

The Anglo-Saxon Chronicle was written several hundred years later and so it gives us only the bare outline of the story.

We do know that the raiders came from across the North Sea, coastal savages of what is now Denmark and North-west Germany and are collectively termed the "Anglo-Saxons".

From 410 A.D. onwards, they had come in their rigged rowing boats, at first making sporadic forays along the coast. The south and south-east coasts of Britain, although further to sail for the Saxons, were the most attractive of all for they were the warmest, most fertile and most civilised. The raiders killed and stole without mercy, setting fire to the farmsteads and seizing valuables, foodstuffs and people (for slaves).

The natives after so many years of peace under Roman rule and protection were ill-equipped to defend themselves. To the Saxon it was a brave adventure and an exciting, and very profitable, escapade. So easy and so profitable in fact, that it soon dawned on them that this island across the sea was a far better place to live in than their own homeland. In 477 A.D. they sailed not to storm and run, but this time, to stay.

The landing was possibly near to Chichester (Cissa's Camp). The three ships were loaded with fighting Saxons, armed and ready for battle. The British fought them off desperately but were mown down by the swords and spears of the invaders. The survivors, the Welsh, fled inland into the refuge of Andredswald.

Another fierce landing is singled out for recording fourteen years later. This time it was even nearer to present-day Lewes, at Pevensey (Anderida) where the dreaded boats invaded again in force. The inhabitants fought back again but, this time, were slaughtered to a man. The Chronicle claims five thousand of them lay dead after the battle, "Aella and Cissa besieged Anderida and killed all who were inside so that there was not one Briton left." The Saxons came in from the sea and took what they could, by the sword, and made themselves "King" of all that they and their kinsmen could hold by terror and by domination.

Sussex became the Kingdom of the South Saxons, hence the final name, "Sussex".

In their colonising they re-carved and re-named the entire countryside. Only a very few names remain in our language today from the "Welsh" of our British ancestors. The-denes, the-fields, the-hursts, the-leys, and the-ings are all Saxon words. The village pattern here in Sussex, as in most of England is the pattern of the Saxon settlement and nearly every single one has a Saxon name. Round Lewes we have: Ham-sey, Off-ham, Well-ing-ham, Souther-ham and Kings-ton, to name only a local handful.

When the red dust of conquest had finally settled, Sussex emerged as a country where Saxon thanes ruled Saxon churls in roughly parcelled village communities, while at the bottom of the social ladder Saxon and surviving "Welsh" slaves toiled out the inevitable harsh existence of the conquered.

Aella, the chieftain who had begun the invasion of Sussex, died in 514 A.D., by which time it is recorded that he was (loosely) head over much of present-day Sussex and Surrey. By this time the country was mainly subdued and his son Cissa succeeded him and, achieved a long and tranquil reign from his centre near Chichester.

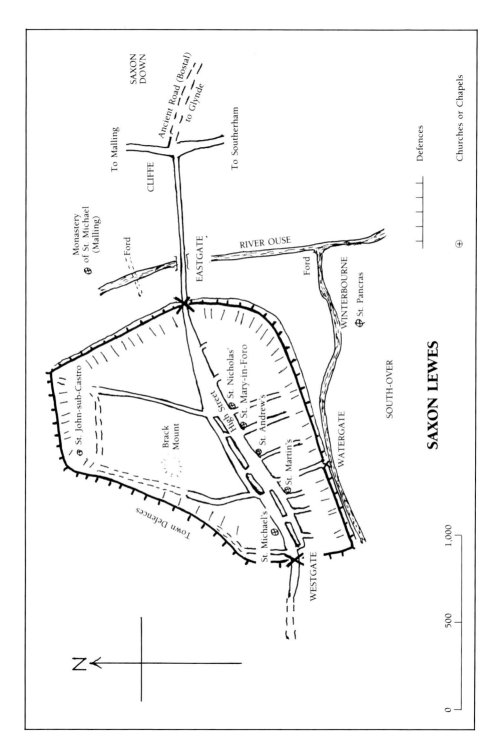

SAXON LEWES

0	500	1,000		Defences
			⊕	Churches or Chapels

SAXON
DOWN

Ancient Road (Bostal)
to Glynde

To Malling

CLIFFE

To Southerham

Monastery
⊕ of St. Michael
(Malling)

Ford

EASTGATE

RIVER OUSE

Ford

WINTERBOURNE

⊕ St. Pancras

St. John-sub-Castro ⊕

Brack
Mount

St. Nicholas'

High Street

⊕ St. Mary-in-Foro

⊕ St. Andrew's

St. Martin's

⊕ St. Martin's

SOUTH-OVER

WATERGATE

Town Defences

St. Michael's ⊕

WESTGATE

N ←

II. SAXON LEWES

On the whole, at first, the Saxons were seldom drawn to towns and town life. They were essentially rugged, rural and sea-faring peoples from the flat, sandy North-German plains. They settled happily on the flat coastal and greensand belt of Sussex. The old ramparts of Caburn were left to further decay and few Saxon villages crowned the chalk hill-country. But a settled country needed defending and Saxon eyes lit unerringly on the lower spur of chalk that cut across the Ouse valley from the escarpment to the river. This was a defence site ideal in every way, not too high above the plain, well-drained, near to the river and easily defended. And so, at last, Lewes was established.

The name derives from the Old English term, "hlaew" meaning "hill". It also means "burial ground". The Saxons did bury their dead on the hills, a famous example of this is at Sutton Hoo, and there are many burial grounds on the downland encircling Lewes, many still awaiting further archaeological research. But for Lewes, "the place on the hill" seems more appropriate.

It is of interest also that, most unusually for the Saxons, the name denotes no particular ownership. Very many of their place-names derived from people with a -ton or -wick etc. added to describe the settlement as outlying or of nearby farmland etc. So it would seem that Lewes, from the first, was not a lordly-owned place or even a large, land-dominating capital town. It was a logically founded settlement, partly for defence and also a useful river-port and market-centre for the exchange of goods and ideas. An unassuming, practical meeting place in fact. One might say that it has still managed to retain much of that character through all the long fourteen centuries of its history.

The Pattern of the Growing Settlement

The original settlement was centred on the flat portion half way up the slope. The "high street" of the 7th century was to become the High Street of the 20th. Feet that tread the shopping street from the Memorial to the "Bottleneck" are walking in the exact footsteps of the rough traders of Saxon times. Parallel to the main thoroughfare were, typically of the Saxon pattern of town settlement, service lanes to the backs of the main line of buildings. Relics of these are still in situ, on the north side the lane is still marked out by Castle Ditch, on the south side, Stewards Inn Lane may mask a similar Saxon service lane.

The dwellings were of timber, rough hewn, with thatched roofs. The thane's house would have stood out as being considerably larger than the others to be used for assemblies, when held, for talk or for feasting. The first buildings would have been scattered but later became coerced into a linear street-plan. Living conditions were primitive. The fire-place, on a stone in the middle of the house, sent its smoke up through a hole in the roof and the windows were mere slits called eye-holes. The floors were beaten earth, sometimes rush-covered and wood furnishings were sparse.

But the Saxons ate and drank with gusto. The land of the plains was cultivated to produce clothing, food and drink. Barley was grown to produce the vast amounts of beer required. The cultivation was of an open pattern with no hedges. It was on a three-field system, one arable, one pasture and one fallow. The fields were very large and cultivated in strips separated only by furrows. One man's holdings were scattered over good and poor land for fair distribution. There was common grazing for the oxen, goats and pigs, the latter particularly grazing on the forest borders for roots and acorns. Sheep grazed on the downland.

The forest was a bountiful source of food beside pasture for the swine. Foxes and wild boar, rabbits and game-birds were plentiful. It was part of the thane's work to organise hunting in the Weald to augment the food supplies. His other responsibility was to be in overall control and to provide defence of his land against enemy attack.

The Saxons of old Lewes were a crude, energetic race. They were ruddy complexioned, blue-eyed and the men were bearded. The clean-shaven face was not introduced until Norman times. They loved bright colours and feasting. At their feasts, in the great rectangular hall of the chief, ale and mead flowed freely and a minstrel bard would sing long into the night of the glory of the fierce battles of their history or the sad legends of their Gods.

As the years went by, the small settlement on the hill extended itself down the spur towards the river, and the wooden stockade, which originally encircled only the flattened centre of the spur, was extended with it to the valley floor. By the end of the Saxon era, it ran from present-day Westgate, up Pipe Passage and around the Castle Mount and the ancient Roman defence-point of St. John-sub-Castro. From there the line ran back along Green Wall to Eastgate, curved along Friar's Walk and Southover Road and up Keere Street back to the High Street.

The highest point of all was Brack Mount, that high, conical hill that sits so unbelievably in the back-garden, indeed it *is* the back-garden of Brack Mound House at the top of Castle Banks. This had always been considered of Saxon construction although it is not entirely typical. It may well have been part of the hastily erected defences of the late Saxons against the next wave of invaders, the Vikings, or it may have been a rather crude first attempt at castle-building by the early Normans. Whoever raised it, it is still an age-old monument to some peoples of long ago who determined that Lewes should be defended to the last.

The Later Saxon Age

The Saxon invaders were pagans, worshipping the old Norse gods and so the Kingdom of the South Saxons stayed heathen and unconverted. It was only rescued from its pagan state after St. Wilfred had made his well-chronicled landing at Selsey another hundred years later in 688 A.D. Indeed, Sussex was the last corner of England to be converted, by which time the countryside around

Lewes had become a pocket of thriving agriculture.

The Saxons, with the sturdy local oxen to drag their heavy two-yoke ploughs through the wealden clay, had begun to push further back the huge forest of oak, ash and thorn. Villages and hamlets dotted the ever-widening fertile plain on the north side of the Downs and Lewes, as the market centre of the area, was becoming a town of craftsmen such as potters, leather-workers, metal-workers and merchant traders.

The central "High Street", now extending to the river, also had many side lanes branching off it at right-angles down the southern slope. Christianity, when at last it had come, had made an incredibly detailed impact on the life of England, even down to influencing the town-plan of Lewes. For now, every one of the side-branching roads (except that to the watergate) was named after a saint, in whose honour a chapel had been built at the top of each lane along the High Street. Today there are still St. Swithun's Terrace, St. Martin's Lane, St. Andrew's Lane and St. Nicholas' Lane all running down from the High Street to the southern foot of the spur. Originally there was also St. Mary's Lane with the church of St. Mary-in-Foro at its head, but this was most unimaginatively renamed Station Street in the throes of Victorian railway enthusiasm. So along the High Street there was now a line of, probably wooden, little churches or

The chancel arch from the previous Church of St. John-sub-Castro with Lombardic lettering commemorating Prince Magnus, the Danish anchorite. Inset is a thirteenth century sepulchral slab. It is now set into the south wall of the present church. The inscription reads, "A Knight of the royal house of Denmark . . . forsook his soldier's life to become a lowly anchorite".

chapels which stood into Medieval times until overshadowed, and finally driven out of existence, by the huge Norman Priory of St. Pancras.

It is impossible to date accurately the foundation of the larger churches of Saxon Lewes. The Saxons built mainly in wood and this was over built in all cases in stone later. The Church of St. Michael in the High Street is thought to have been established under the auspices of the Saxon monastery in Malling in late Saxon times as was All Saints Church at the foot of the southern slope.

The churchyard site of the church of St. John-sub-Castro is almost certainly older than both these. Its northern wall now rears up in cathedral-like porportions from St. John's Hill. The stone south doorway, incorporated into the later ages of recurrent building, dates from Saxon times. Moreover, on the outside south wall of the old nave, is a unique relic of the same age that proclaims, in Latin letters, "A knight of the royal house of Denmark . . . forsook his soldier's life to become a lowly anchorite", and presumably ended up his days, as a change from hacking and murdering, peacefully viewing the ever-developing countryside along the Ouse valley and the unending forest barrier beyond.

To Christianity and the Saxons we also owe our parish boundaries, delineated at this time. So Lewes was laid out and developed to Saxon requirements, and so it has remained to this day.

Across the Ouse, the early Church had proved even more extensively powerful. A huge block of land, extending from modern Tunbridge Wells in the north to Beddingham in the south was granted to Christchurch Canterbury in the early 9th century. In 838 the gift was ratified by King Aethelwulf. It also included 21 Lewes haws or holdings. So the Church controlled all of Malling and along the riverside to Southerham, and all the country north of this including Wellingham, Glynde, Isfield, Little Horsted, Uckfield, Framfield, Mayfield, Rotherfield and Wadhurst. A huge estate. It was administered from the Archbishop's palace at Mayfield and from the Benedictine St. Michael's monastery at Malling. This had previously been founded by King Ealdwulf's gift to his thegn Hunlaf, with land appertaining to it scattered as far as Ditchling, Lindfield (directly up the Ouse) and Chiddingly.

During this time, Lewes continued to develop peacefully. The forests of the Weald, the Andredswald, kept it well out of the continuous battles for supremacy that swept Mercia, Anglia and the North. Trade by river and by the rough roads developed. The surrounding supportive land increased in production in its Saxon-owned Manors or Hundreds (approximately a hundred farms or hides) and the forest continued to be very slowly pushed back by laborious clearance.

The Danish Invasions 853 A.D.

But as England became more settled and more productive, so she again became more attractive to raiders from the harsher lands across the North Sea. This time the invasion came from the coast lands of the Norwegian fiords and, again, Denmark.

We have no written records of the fate of Lewes during these years. North of the Thames, the Vikings, or "Danes" as they came to be collectively called, wreaked havoc far and wide, ravaging the countryside and plundering the rich treasures of the monasteries all down the East Coast of Saxon England. The "fury of the Norseman" became a watchword of terror and the storm raged for over a hundred years.

Like the Saxons before them, they came to rob but stayed to conquer. Within half a century they had taken, and now ruled, the greater part of England. Only parts of Wessex (which now included Sussex) at one time stood unconquered. Into Wessex the Danes attacked from the Isle of Wight and from Hastings, but Lewes is not specifically mentioned in the Anglo-Saxon Chronicle for the time.* It must have undoubtedly come under threat for, in 1796, a horde of buried coins was dug up at Offham, only one and a half miles inland from Lewes, which date from this time. A sign of great fear and hurried flight on the part of some Saxon inhabitant.

It is a fact that five times the number of buried hordes have been unearthed dating between 870 and 880 A.D. than from any other years in the long history of our island.

The flood-tide of the Danes was only stemmed when Alfred the Great inherited the Kingdom of Wessex from his brothers. He rallied his demoralised subjects to fight the enemy with their own weapons. It was from them that he learned the advantage of having solid centres for defence and shelter. Wessex towns, Lewes among them, were ringed about by stoneworks to augment the previous wooden barriers. Around Lewes, these would have been of chalk and flint.

The army, or fryd, was reorganised. The thegn, if he owned over 600 acres, was called to be the permanent defender of his lands and assigned to military service at all times. Of the free-men, half were called up for service and half were left to farm the land.

The defended towns were known as "burghs", a Viking name. Those within easy reach of the coast, such as Lewes, had the added responsibility of contributing to the new navy of ships organised by the king, to intercept the raiders at sea.

In the "Burghal Hidage", a written document on defence, of Alfred's reign, Lewes was adjudged to have a total of 300 hides. A hide of defence was the amount of land needed to provide for one family, and the hidage was the amount of land needed to provide sufficient men to defend the town wall. Lewes' hidage gives an estimated length of her enclosing wall as around 5,000 feet, almost

---

* *Heneage Legge quotes a repulsed Danish attack locally in the "21st year of King Alfred's reign" in Fabian's Chronicle.*

a mile. This, as a circuit, would fit snugly around the spur from Eastgate to Westgate.

Alfred also learned the "shire" and "county" divisions of land from the Danes and sub-divided his kingdom accordingly. Lewes was now placed as being in the Shire of Sussex in the Kingdom of Wessex.

Locally, Beddingham and Rotherfield are both mentioned in King Alfred's will. Alfriston and Westdean are also associated with him. The name Kingston, the village now adjacent to Lewes to the south, derives from "The place where the King's taxes are collected". In the century following, Lewes is mentioned as having been given to Earl Godwin, the father of King Harold, the last of the Saxon kings.

Under King Alfred's determined leadership Wessex finally drove the invaders across her borders for good and a clear cut boundary was established by Alfred and Guthrum's Peace.

But all strength and unity depended on the strength of the ruler. When a weak king, Ethelred the Redeless, succeeded in 985 the longboats of the Danes again appeared off the coasts of Britain. In 1009 A.D., the Anglo-Saxon Chronicle records the marauding advance of the Norsemen through Kent, Sussex and Hampshire, riding on their stolen ponies, west from the Kent coast and forging east from the Isle of Wight. Etheldred's attempts to buy the Norsemen off with money brought far-reaching changes to the country's economical system. The sums demanded were enormous. Up to 1006 A.D., one hundred thousand pounds in gold and silver had been paid over. The money was raised by a tax on land known as the Dane-Geld, the first such tax known in that form, in England, and the beginning of our present fiscal system.

The money had to be minted, and Burghs such as Lewes were granted powers to mint the money needed and also to be centres for collecting it from the surrounding shires. By King Athelstan's reign, Lewes had already possessed two mints. By the end of the 10th century she was recognised, in official documents, as an "urbs" which denoted her as a principal town, and she was stamping "Lae urb" on her minted coinage. Later she could boast of having nineteen moneyers.

By the reign of Edward the Confessor, Lewes was recorded as possessing fifteen moniers among the one hundred and twenty burgesses. At the same time it was required to contribute twenty shillings for coastal defence whenever needed. Economically, Lewes was obviously a port, a fiscal centre and a market-town of considerable standing. The drain on the country in paying the Dane-geld had been made good under the peace of Edward and his predecessor the Danish King Canute.

It was in this prosperous period that Saxon building in stone, particularly of churches, became more widespread. St. John-sub-Castro was likely to have been rebuilt at this time, the relics of which can still be seen. In the countryside too, there were developments. Water-mills had been invented for grinding corn and were now in use on the Sussex rivers. Two were sited along the Winterbourne in later years and may have existed at this time. Along the Ouse there were more. Windmills were not introduced until the Norman period.

Salt-pans would also have contributed to the wealth of Lewes. In the Domesday Survey, 285 salt-pans are listed in Sussex. A relic of these is undoubtedly the "Dripping-pan" field behind Mountfield Road on the sea-ward side of the town. Salt was vital for salting meat and fish to preserve them for the winter food supplies.

In the forests of the Weald, the primitive iron-industry had been revived. Now water supplied power as well as wood in the form of charcoal. The Saxons became workers of fine metal goods, not only for weapons but also for brooches, buckles, jewellery and drinking and eating vessels. The iron for the wealthy was overlaid with gold, silver, jewels and enamels.

Besides the moneyers, some of the burgesses of Lewes were craftsmen in metal, wood or leather or fine woollen goods. All these derived from materials produced in the surrounding countryside. Others would have been merchants trading around the south and east coasts of Britain or across the seas with European ports.

Many of them would have also been owners of surrounding manors, on the plain and on the Downs, still farmed on the open-field system. Here, the narrow half-acre strips across the huge fields were worked by "cottars" or "bordars" who paid rent in work or in kind to the man next above him in the social scale. He, in his turn, owed duties and allegiance, with the "villani" of larger holdings, to the Lord of the Manor.

Along the Ouse Valley, manors had become sizeable villages. Rodmell and Iford had over a hundred dwellings each. Southease and Bishopstone had slightly less. Malling, in the Domesday Survey, is written as larger than Lewes itself, but this estimate covered the whole area owned by the Church of Canterbury which stretched from Southerham to Mayfield. Other nearby villages were Firle, Beddingham, and, inland, Hamsey, Plumpton and Barcombe.

In the countryside, the landless were serfs or slaves, usually servants to the bigger landowners of the manor. In the town they could work themselves up to a respected, but menial, position in a craft, or as a servant in the town dwelling house.

The pattern was one of security and allegiance and over-all contentment of the average Saxon with his lot. Compared with countries elsewhere in the Western world, England was a pleasant, peaceful and productive land. It was also an attractive one and, this time, all the wealth of the kingdom could not buy off the last and greatest threat in her history from the Norsemen across the seas.

The onslaught, when it came, stemmed not from the old Norwegian and Danish homelands of the North, but from Vikings who had settled into greater prosperity in north-west France, now known as the Normans. Their leader was a fierce fighter, William, now known as William the Conqueror.

William of Normandy was a warrior king who boasted that he waged a fighting campaign every single year of his adult life. His adult life began at the age of fourteen and ended when he was sixty, throughout which time he must, indeed, have created a mountainous harvest of suffering and misery through his insatiable thirst for war. In 1066 A.D. he turned his eyes westwards and, with the cold, meticulous precision for which he was already famed, he plotted the invasion of England.

III. THE NORMAN CONQUEST

William landed his troops along the Sussex shore at Pevensey, re-fortified it, and also occupied neighbouring Hastings with which he already had social, religious and economic links. He then marched up the sandstone ridge to meet and annihilate King Harold's Saxon army at Battle.

Lewes was providentially by-passed in the invasion, sited so snugly six to eight miles in from the Channel, up the Ouse estuary and nestled in downland and forest. But she had sent her quota in men and money to support her king and for this she would have to pay the price of the loser.

But it soon dawned upon the whole countryside that everybody was going to have to pay — and pay — and pay, especially Sussex since it was now on the main highway between King William, centred in London, and his homeland of Normandy just across the water.

Sussex came under the iron hand of Norman reorganisation immediately.

The old Saxon feudal system of land tenure was retained. Why not? It made the re-organisation so much more simple for the new king. The machinery for land-owning, service giving and tax-gathering was already established countrywide. All the change required was for it to be given over, lock, stock and barrel, to all the Norman lords who had followed William. They would hold all the land directly from him. The shires were kept intact, as were the burghs and the old Saxon manorial villages. Their old lords, if they had not been killed in the Battle, were summarily dispossessed and replaced by Norman lords and overlords.

Sussex was over-all divided, for further safety, into Rapes. Five in all, like many of the parishes of old, they ran lengthwise north to south, each covering the different bands of countryside: Downland, sand and clay plain, Wealden forest and birch-covered High Weald. The Lewes Rape stretched from the Ouse westward to the Adur at Shoreham and north to Ifield. To detail the size, take the A275 road north from Lewes as far as East Grinstead. Here turn west (left) for Crawley. From here drop south again all the way back to the coast at Shoreham. All the land then encompassed is the approximate extent of the Rape of Lewes.

Under Norman rule Lewes suddenly found itself not only in the front line, as a south coast port little more than fifty miles from Normandy, but also a capital city of one fifth of the shire of Sussex. The Norman fist tightened its hold still further. The Lordship of the Rape was given to a sterling supporter of the Norman cause, Earl William de Warenne, who immediately set about building a solid castle to defend his property. Moreover he sited his castle in the very heart of the old town of Lewes.

The Saxon houses and cottages, probably fifty or more, were ruthlessly demolished and swept away to make room for the stronghold. First a temporary, wooden structure for defence was erected on the Brack mount. But by the end of the century the permanent stone keep as we know it today had been built. This was perched high on a new mound of chalk and earth dug from the surrounding, excavated, ditch. At the back of the north side of Lewes High Street one can still walk along part of the ditch and see the, much restored, curtain walls of the castle towering above.

On the west side of the castle, the Normans utilised the old Saxon wall defences and built them up to the almost sheer face that can still be seen along Westgate Street. To follow the strength of the defences on this side, one can turn off the High Street along Pipe Passage and tread the ancient walk of both Saxon and Norman sentinels which now skirts the castle.

At first the shell keep of stone, chalk and flint formed a simple, circular enclosure. The guard towers, probably three eventually, were added two hundred years later. The whole area was surrounded by a strong Bailey (or Curtain) stone

Lewes Castle keep towers above the timber-framed Castle Antiques off the High Street.

wall which can still be seen today around the car-park adjoining the bowling-green, much repaired now and restored. The present bowling-green was the gathering and tourney-ground for the castle.

The original Norman Gatehouse had the addition of a very imposing Barbican Gate in the early fourteenth century. This is of much finer workmanship than the original castle buildings, being finished with a careful covering of dressed or knapped flints. It is, in fact, one of the finest barbicans in the country and the double gateway forms a splendid entrance to the castle site.

As a fortification, the castle would certainly have made its threatening point of Norman superiority to the Saxon townsfolk and the dwellers in the countryside, especially as they had been forced to provide all the labour for its building. The keep measures thirty-eight feet across. As a dwelling for a lord and his lady wife, Grundrada, it looks cold and cramped to modern eyes although there would have been additional store-houses and stables etc. within the bailey.

William de Warenne had many other possessions in England and owned property in twelve counties altogether with castles also at Reigate and Castle Acre in Norfolk. However, of all these, Lewes is said to have been his favourite residence. He and his successors were the only members of the aristocracy who could claim a practical overlordship of Lewes at any time. His name, and that of his wife, are commemorated in the Gundreda and De Warenne Roads on the Wallands Park Estate. To the second Earl, his son, the town owes its chequered coat of arms. These were those of his wife Isabel, a lady he boldly eloped with some time before the actual demise of her first husband.

After nine hundred years a considerable amount of the castle building still remains, but of the other De Warenne foundation, the magnificent St. Pancras Priory of Lewes, there is hardly a trace.

The Priory

It takes a great deal of imagination now to picture the towers and the lofty roofs of the vast Cluniac priory soaring above the modest roof-line of the present suburb of Southover. The whole priory site covered thirty acres of land that is now games fields, nursery gardens and sad, scattered ruins. Here William de Warenne and his lady wife built one of the greatest religious foundations in the land. Its glorious church, dedicated to St. Pancras in honour of a small Saxon church formerly on the site, outspaced even Chichester Cathedral. It was nearly a tenth of a mile long.

Its walls were faced with the finest Caen stone. The graceful arches and columns everywhere bore a wealth of delicate carvings. Its twin towers, two hundred feet high, rivalled the lofty height of the castle on its mount. Cloisters, fraters, the Chapter-house, Infirmary and dorter (the largest in all England) spread a further four hundred feet to the south.

Drive along the Lewes By-pass and look across at the little town and picture a set of buildings spread around a second Canterbury Cathedral occupying all the land between the by-pass and the edge of the town. For this is how it must have appeared.

The story of its foundation has been preserved in its charter. William and Gundrada were travelling across Burgundy on their way to Rome when they were held up by local warfare. They turned to the nearby monastery for shelter and were given an honourable welcome at the Cluniac Abbey of St. Peter, founded in 910 A.D. in an effort to bring more discipline to the original Benedictine Rule.

They were so impressed by the Cluniac Order and the hospitality it had afforded them, that they immediately turned back for home and insisted on four of the French monks coming to Lewes to help establish a priory of the same order at Lewes on the open land at Southover.

The entrance to the Priory was through a majestic two-storied gateway off the (then) Juggs Lane, the ancient trackway that ran over Kingston Ridge and across the Downs to Brighthelmstone and was used by the fisher-women to bring in panniers (juggs) on their donkeys each week. Juggs Lane now starts at the western end of Southover High Street at its junction with Bell Lane. When the Lewes by-pass was cut through it, it was allocated a magnificent rainbow arch to fling it across the new road. How impressed the old fisher folk would have been, and full marks to the County Engineers for their imaginative building.

The sad remains of the larger arch of the Priory gateway can now be seen along the Southover High Street between Priory Crescent and St. John's Church. It was built of Sussex marble, a hard conglomerate much prized in this area. To visualise its original magnificence one must drive to Battle and see the gateway to Battle Abbey which has a similar two-arched construction and still stands in all its original glory.

The Church of St. John the Baptist alongside, is all that usefully remains of the once great priory. Sited as it was, alongside the great Priory entrance, it was presumably the guest-house or Hospitium of the Priory and, no doubt, the exact replica of that monastic guest-house in Burgundy that had inspired William de Warenne to his rich endowment. Building was started in 1077 and the first Prior, Lanzo, appointed from France. It continued for two hundred years under sixteen successive French priors until the final twin towers were added to the church around 1268 and all was complete. In the meantime it had acquired a great deal of land and property in the surrounding countryside and also holdings in Lewes. It brought much prestige to the town and possibly wealth. Whether the townsfolk as a body had friendly feelings towards their impressive neighbour is not recorded. They had accepted, tight lipped, their Norman overlord and his retainers, these foreigners who spoke in an altogether different language (French) and crippled them with endless taxation. To them, the Priory must have seemed just one more Norman imposition, another tax-collector and another unwelcome intruder, although it undoubtedly gave employment locally and much needed hospitality to travellers.

As the local Cluniac authority grew, in religious as well as social importance, so the town's established Saxon chapels diminished and, one by one, became impoverished and deserted. At the beginning of the 14th century there were fourteen churches in Lewes, ten of which stood within the walls. In 1337 these were summarily reduced to four, St. Michael's, St. John-sub-Castro, All Saints and St. Andrew's.

However, the people of Lewes made full use of the feast day inaugurated in honour of St. Pancras on May 12th as a public holiday. They never failed to enjoy the excuse for thronging the streets in procession and rowdy celebration.

Like the Lords of the castle, the Prior had many privileges, usually at the expense of the townsfolk. For example, in 1089 we read that he had been granted the right to first choice of goods, after William de Warenne, at the town's daily provision market "for themselves and for the maintaining of the guest-house". The Priory also had its share in the taxes on trade at the town's markets and fairs.

The Priory guest-house, like all the religious houses, provided shelter for all wayfarers. It gave board and lodging for those travelling down from the north on the road that ran through Malling, over Cliffe Bridge and through the suburb of Southover, and also to those journeying on the road that ran south, through Chailey to enter Lewes through the Westgate. Even shelter for the poor and sick was provided for and the Priory would have been responsible for tending those in the St. Nicholas' Hospital, outside the town on the latter road, which was founded and endowed by William de Warenne.

The only relics of this hospital now are the name "spital" given to the triangle where the London Road turns sharply from south to east to enter the top of the town, and also in the old name for the field opposite, behind Lewes Gaol, which was known as Spital Field.

A second hospital was built by the monks of the Priory in the 14th century at the time of the Black Death. This was the St. James' Hospital just outside the Priory gateway in Southover. This may have replaced one within the Priory precincts. Only the chapel of this hospital now remains. It stands as a fine, untouched, example of 14th century architecture opposite the Southover Grange.

In addition to providing nursing care and medicines for travellers and the local people, the Priory would have offered education for the sons of the noble houses in the area. A grammar school, run by the Priory, is recorded as early as 1248 and, even when the first non-religious Grammar School was founded in Southover in 1512, one of the trustees to be appointed was the Prior of St. Pancras Priory.

Lastly, the Priory provided a noble resting place for the local aristocratic families of Norman birth. Most of the de Warennes in succession were buried in the Priory church, as were their successors, two Earls of Arundel and their wives and, later, George Neville, Lord Abergavenny. The Lady Gundrada died

Ruins of the Norman Priory of St. Pancras founded by William de Warenne and his wife, Gundrada, in the eleventh century. Destroyed under Henry VIII in 1537.

at their Norfolk castle, Castle Acre, but her body was brought back to Lewes for burial.

While the Norman kingly line was in the ascendant in England, the French Cluniac authority predominated at the Priory. But as the ties between England and France slackened over the centuries, the French speaking, French controlled Priory lost popularity. That it openly and actively took the part of Henry III and his French queen against the anti-French champion, Simon de Montfort, reduced its standing still further. During the Hundred Years War that dragged on through the 14th and 15th centuries, Frenchmen, as the enemy, were even less welcome in England and the King's Charter cut the ties between Cluniac Lewes and the mother-house in Burgundy altogether.

By the end of the 14th century, the priory, at last, had English priors, John Oke, Thomas Neland and, last of all, Robert Croham. By this time the number of monks had been reduced to only twenty four from the original sixty. We do not have any concrete evidence, good or bad, of the influence of the individual Father Priors on the town. One of them, John de Charlieu, showed a local patriotism in 1377, during the Hundred Years War, in helping to fight off a raid of Frenchmen on the South Coast. Alas, he was taken prisoner in the fight and his ransom may have only added another tax burden to the town for all his good intentions.

The end came with the Dissolution of the monasteries under Henry in 1537.

There is something almost sinister in the furious vengeance Thomas Cromwell, the King's Chancellor, wreaked upon the Priory of St. Pancras. Was it purely a hatred for everything French or ecclesiastic, or had Cromwell received some personal snub from the foundation at some time? We shall never know. What we do know is that his orders for demolition here, were more ferocious than at any other site in the land. His engineer for the demolition, John Portinari, has left detailed accounts of how each wall was undermined. Thick baulks of wood were thrust through holes at ground level, and these were then set on fire, to bring every single lovingly carved wall, archway and pillar crashing to earth.

On a grey morning in November 1537 the demolition team of eighteen moved in. Within eight or nine days the four hundred year old Priory was literally razed to the ground. All that remained were a few stumps of outer walls and the Prior's house which Cromwell retained for his own use when the estate was given to him, by the King, as the crowning reward for his services.

Also left were the dove-cot, said to hold over three thousand birds, and the Hospitium which is now St. John's Church. The beautiful Priory church was almost completely obliterated. The cherished graves of the nobility were crudely trampled upon, together with the High altar, fine brasses, and carvings — everything was gone.

The townsfolk of Lewes were quick to pounce on the pickings. They all, with one accord, built or repaired their houses with the stones from the ruins. Local belief has it that every house in Lewes dating from the 16th century has at least one stone taken from the Priory ruins, in its structure. In the lower High Street, now a shopping precinct, buildings on the north side are thought to be faced with Priory stone. In Southover, the Red House has carved stones built into its cellars. Much of Anne of Cleves House used Priory stone. The Grange was built, in 1572, almost entirely from the material of the Lord's Place, the re-modelled Prior's House appropriated to his own use by Thomas Cromwell and later destroyed by fire.

Looking at the ruined site today, it is almost as though Cromwell's malevolence still blights it. However his own fall from power and execution followed swiftly. Or does the curse, to be found in the original Priory Charter of William de Warenne, still haunt the lonely stones? "May God meet there, those who oppose and destroy these (buildings), with the sword of anger, fury and vengeance and eternal malediction".

Not here is the loving care devoted to Wilmington Priory, or the impeccable presentation of Bayham Abbey. In Lewes, the Priory ruins lie shattered and forlorn. A putting green encroaches the ruins of the Infirmary Hall, and a bowling green adjoins it, while on the far side, tennis courts threaten to engulf every deserted inch of remaining ground.

In 1847, the Victorians added the crowning insult by carving a huge gash diagonally through the entire site to bring the railway from Brighton to Lewes. It drove a deep cleft right through the former chancel of the great church. In a most unexpected way it became a blessing in disguise as, incredible to relate, the caskets containing the bones of the founders, William de Warenne and Lady Gundrada, came up to the light again, after lying lost for three hundred years. A modern chapel was built for them attached to Southover Church and the original black burial stone, which had already been retrieved from its refuge on the Shurley tomb in Isfield church in 1775, was set to cover the new tomb.

The rest of the Priory Church ruins and the adjoining cloister foundations now lie north of the railway where they have become rubbish dumps in part of a nursery-garden establishment. However, there is a small, almost hidden, public tunnel, which provides a path under the railway at the west end of the remains of the Frater, so that this part of the ruins can still be traced within the precincts of the nursery.

Interestingly, the most evocative corner of these sad ruins, is the remains of the Infirmary chapel. Here the shapes of the two side chapels are most clearly defined and also the remains of the main altar. Is it just coincidence that this little chapel was most probably built over that original, humble chapel dedicated to St. Pancras that was founded, long before the Norman Conquest, outside Saxon Lewes?

Alongside the Priory site, and an excellent viewing point, is the Mount. Another mystery, for there are no records extant to tell when or why it was built. It obviously made, and still does, a useful calvary, 45 feet high, so near to the Priory. However it probably owes its existence to the fact that it is alongside the Dripping Pan, the next field running east, which is a flat, sunken area undoubtedly a relic of the salt-pans of old. Such mounds and pans together are to be seen again in Essex, where it is thought the mounds may have been surmounted by windmills. This field, the Mount and the adjoining Convent Field were presented to the town, by Mr Aubrey Hillman of Saxonbury in Southover in 1895 for the recreation of the towns-people.

The Dripping Pan is now a football ground along Mountfield Road and, south of it, the Convent (originally "Priory") Field is a cricket ground. Along with the time-honoured bowling-green at the castle, one might say that the town at least puts its relics to healthy use!

In tracing the history of the Priory to its untimely end we have deviated far beyond the story of the town as it settled down warily under its Norman conquerors. Let us return there, from Southover, and continue our search into its Norman past.

IV. NORMAN AND MEDIEVAL LEWES

The Saxon town in 1066 was a compact unit, neatly defended by a town wall encircling three sides of the spur. Estimates give the population as somewhere between one and two thousand for the entire urban area, which would have included dwellings in the suburbs of Westout to the west and Cliffe to the east.

In the Domesday reckoning, the Borough of Lewes had 127 burgesses. Cliffe is enumerated separately as it lay in the neighbouring rape of Pevensey. Here, the Book registered 39 inhabited dwellings and twenty that were uninhabited. Why so many houses were registered empty is a mystery. Some might have been of people killed in battle, but then, again, they might only have been flooded out! Cliffe was perpetually being covered with water at high tide. Or the inhabitants may have moved into the fast growing town across the river, for Lewes was growing rapidly around its imposing castle.

Strong gateways straddled the two road entrances to the town from the east and the west. East Gate stood at the bottom of present-day School Hill looking towards the bridge over the Ouse. The area is still known as Eastgate, as is the chapel nearby, built in Victorian times. The western entrance was the most vulnerable point in the town defences. Here, the neck of the spur runs straight off the Downland behind it and there is little physical barrier to aid defence. Well-planned attack would always come from the west as Simon de Montfort demonstrated in 1264.

When they strengthened the town walls with new stone, the Normans built a formidable West Gate to defend this entrance to the town. We still have complete details of the work. The fortress-like entrance stood four-square across the High Street, its inner wall coinciding with the present west wall of the entrance to the Westgate Chapel, then the site of the first ale-house to be reached in the town. The gateway itself was truly massive. The central archway constricted traffic to ten feet across but the arch itself was fifteen feet deep. On either side of this were twin towers, rounded on their outward sides, each thirty feet across and thirty feet deep. The remains of the northern tower is still to be seen in the present Freemason's Hall at this spot. It was used, for many years, as a prison cell for the town's law-breakers. A similar gateway, still standing, is the Landgate of Rye.

The Watergate stood at the bottom of Watergate Lane, by the side of the Winterbourne inlet. Possibly this was more in the nature of a postern gate. No relic of it now remains except the naming of the street.

New flint and stone town walls, built by the Normans and later reinforced, joined all three gates to the west end of the town and to the south and then swung northwards, via the present Greenwall, to enclose St. John-sub-Castro, Brack Mount and the castle, as the lighter walling had in Saxon times. There is no continuous walk along the length of the walls as there is, for example in Chester, but there are still many traces of them to be found, particularly in Westgate Street, along Pipe Passage and at the west side of St. John's Church. Relics of the original construction can also be seen along the east side of Keere Street. Here, the entrenched remains of a huge rampart of chalk and flint is fronted by an outer ditch in which the houses, and their gardens, stand.

Turning left at the foot of the street, one can climb up behind the walls, now much modernised and strengthened, and look south over them, from the bottom of St. Swithun's Terrace, as did the defenders of old. The houses on the steep slope behind the wall here occupy the area that was formerly the town orchard. A well chosen site for it, south-facing and with excellent drainage.

The Housing 1100-1500

The area within the repaired or reconstructed walls filled up with a complete network of lanes and dwellings. From this time we can date the "twittens" which are unique to Sussex. These are the narrow alley-ways that link up the official roads in a manner most convenient to the pedestrian. The name, it is suggested, derives from "betwixt and between". Brooman's Lane, Walwers Lane and Church Twitten still lead from School Hill down to the foot of the spur, but there are many more twittens such as Pipe Passage, Green Lane and Pope's Entry, to name a few. They are rarely fronted by houses and all are walled usually with flint or stone.

The houses in Norman and Medieval times were either of rough wooden construction or timber-framed, in-filled with lath and plaster. The roofs were thatched or of wood. Later, tiles took the place of thatch to guard against the ever-present risk of fire. Flint, also, became popular for wall construction, particularly for the churches.

At the top of St. Martin's Lane there is a beautifully preserved relic of early Medieval Lewes in the date 1330 against the side of the building beneath the wooden tracery.

Shops usually consisted of the front room of the house-owner or a stall placed in the roadway just outside, selling whatever the craftsman of the house, and his apprentices if he had them, produced - shoes or cloth, candles, platters and bowls, leather goods, gloves etc.

Underfoot in the houses was beaten earth or rushes. Along the main street the surface came to be cobbled or stone-covered. There was always a good supply of pebbles along the beaches of the Sussex coast. A drain ran down the street, either in the centre or at both sides. In either case it was a running cess-pit of rubbish and dirt, animal remains and general filth.

But the Medieval towns-folk did not live exclusively shut away in their towns. The craftsman and the merchant all owned land in the surrounding countryside, even if it was only grazing and stabling for his horses. Country and town were still interwoven in an inseparable bond.

Administration and Trade

Although the town was officially administered by the Norman overlord and the local burghers, the maintenance of the town was a communal business. There were no rights without duties. If the town wall or ditch needed repairing, the townsfolk provided the labour. When the town fields called for harvesting, the townsfolk became the farm-workers.

Lewes gained a charter of some independence very early on in Norman times. In 1148, in the troubled reign of Stephen, this was ratified by the 4th Earl de Warenne, Reginald, who: "Restored to the Burgesses of Lewes a Merchant Guild, with all customs and dignities which belong to the same . . . for twenty shillings to be paid yearly to the provostry of Lewes". It must have been very satisfying for the burghers of Lewes. As wealth increased, so the houses of the merchant class enlarged until, in the later Middle Ages, the first storey overhung the ground-floor in a "jetty". The shape of these can still be picked out down the building-line along the High Street and along the north side of the Cliffe.

There would be even more traces of Old Lewes if one could dig down under the buildings of today. The Saxon chapels, for instance, had their stone crypts in the soft chalk below and the whole of Lewes High Street is much-tunnelled with old passages and cellars.

Above ground the market town was thriving. The market took place in the High Street, the market-cross stood outside the present-day Barbican House. Here the town crier would spread the news and ordinances. The town well stood near the War Memorial where the church of St. Nicholas still occupied a central site in the street. On Saturdays, the weekly market occupied all the level ground, cattle at one side, sheep at the other. The animals came in on the hoof, up the steep, cobbled hill from the bridge across the Ouse, or passing through the suburb of St. Anne's Westout and through the massive West Gate.

Their owners were promptly required to pay dues for the privilege of entering the gates and, again, on their profits within the market. Most of these dues went to the Prior and to the King via the current Lord. This did not stop the farmers and traders enjoying their market day. There was a good supply of ale-houses, starting with the Bull Inn at the West Gate, to help the day along. In fact, Lewes, at one time, boasted more hostelries and ale-houses than any other town in Sussex.

There was day to day marketing for all the produce of the surrounding countryside: vegetables, poultry, wool and woven goods and tools etc. Among the town's house and shop-holders we have written record of:- Adam the Girdler, Maurice the Glass-wright, Robert the Hafter (a haft is a tool handle) and Andrew the Brewer. There were no surnames in Medieval times.

The merchants and craftsmen were organised into guilds. We have the record of the Guild of St. Sebastian (bowmen perhaps) in the time of Edward III in the 14th century, but the town books for this period have been lost so we have little other detailed knowledge of the guilds of the town at that time.

All was administered by the chief burgesses who functioned under the town Sheriff (originally the shire-reeve). There was a separate Sheriff to administer the Rape for the Lord. The domestic side of the castle was run by the Steward, commemorated by Stewards Inn Lane just across the High Street from the castle.

Justice in the town was meted out at the Court of the Borough at Michelmas. The offences sound very familiar:- Selling underweight, putting rubbish (and offal) on the highroads, selling unwholesome food, cases of debt, cases of assault. Fines came to the town with shares milked off by the Prior and also by the Archbishop of Canterbury who still held the huge parish of Malling and the patronage of the newly-founded St. Michael's Church in Lewes.

Along Abinger Place, between St. John's Church and the castle, stands Gallows Bank. A fading stone plaque on the wall commemorates the site of the town gallows. It was, as is the tradition, "outside the city walls". It stood by the present Elephant and Castle at the entrance to the town from the Landport Levels. The stocks were here too, and the town (formerly manor) pound for straying livestock.

Across the Offham Road, alongside Paddock Road, lies Hangman's Acre, now a more prosaic stretch of allotments in the corner of the Paddock Field. This was the prerequisite of the hangman but, when hanging went out of fashion, it returned to town ownership.

But the town developed no further in this direction. Expansion was primarily directed down the main slope of the spur, present-day School Hill, and across the river into Cliffe, in the neighbouring rape. For Lewes was enlarging wonderfully as a port. Waterways were always far more convenient, where possible, than any sort of land transport, especially for goods traffic.

We forget just how tediously difficult and thoroughly uncomfortable coach or cart transport always was. Wealden lanes have been notorious, all through history, for their impassable nature. In Sussex, bullocks were invariably used for hauling anything on wheels because of the heavy, thick mud which no horse could cope with.

There is the famous local story, told in an entrancing Sussex accent, of the unfortunate traveller who was espied sinking up to his neck in the mud along the highway. He was hauled to safety by the heroic exertions of a timely passer-by and roughly cleaned into some sort of recognition, only to splutter protestingly, "But you've left my horse down there. I was sitting on him!"

If you find that hard to believe, try walking, even now, down any bridle path south of Uckfield or Heathfield at any time of the year except after a six-week drought!

Fortunately, all the main rivers of Sussex run north to south. The Ouse was always much in demand for transport. It was navigable for smaller vessels as far as Lindfield. It is tidal as far as Barcombe. There was also the turn off up the

Winterbourne past the Watergate of Lewes and, to the east, the tributary reaches of Glynde and Ringmer.

As Lewes prospered under the Normans, so did its port grow busy and rich. Merchants came from far and wide. Ships plied round from London and other smaller ports of south and east England. Wine from Gascony flooded in to grace the tables of the wealthy. The Flemings brought fine cloth, the French tapestries. There were mirrors, muslin, spices and the inevitable salt and fish.

Surplus corn and malt, metal goods, leather and timber were transported out, but the main export very soon became wool from the sheep grazing the rounded, downland hills. In the 13th and 14th centuries, wool became pre-eminent. It was exported raw to the Low Countries for spinning and weaving. Edward I collected huge dues on the trade, with a duty of 20 shillings on each sixpenny bale. No wonder smuggling was the inevitable outcome. Wool smugglers were known as "owlers". So Lewes, along with the rest of Sussex, took her first lessons in contraband connivance.

Along the river were also timber yards and boat yards for building the smaller craft. The timber came down, by water, from the upper reaches of the Ouse and, together with the demands of the iron industry, deforested the backing Wealden forest. In Tudor times one ship of the line took two thousand oaks to build, and it was the Weald that supplied them.

In the later Middle Ages also, culminating to a peak in Tudor times, came iron from the forests of the Weald. Again the river, to the port of Lewes and to the open sea beyond, was invaluable for transport. It is hard to imagine the Weald as the Black Country of England, but so it was from the 13th to the 16th or even 17th centuries.

Iron ore is widespread in the Tunbridge Wells Sands. It had been worked almost since the dawn of history. The early Saxons, initially ignored it, for theirs was a world of wood or fine metals. But, with the Normans, the Iron Age was resumed. With their chain-mail and their armed horses, iron was an essential. In the 13th century we have record of an order to the Sheriff of Sussex for 30,000 iron horse-shoes for the royal troops, together with 60,000 nails. Later, in 1264, a toll was levied of one penny on every cart entering Lewes carrying iron for sale.

Lying across the bridge, in the narrow valley between Lewes town and Caburn, the business of the whole of the Cliffe suburb was centred upon the river and its trading. A few yards downstream from the bridge the river bends east and runs directly behind the south side of the Main Street. The houses on this side backed right down to the water with its continuing line of yards and warehouses. It bends again, to back the housing along South Street, where there were chandlers, ale-houses, the Bargemaster's House (the name is still in use) and more boat yards. South Street then was the road south out of Lewes and now continues as a riverside path where once the way led to Southerham and to Seaford.

Looking back from a short walk southwards along this path will afford an unexpectedly interesting view. Along the river bank, behind South Street, the boat yard of the Lewes Boating Club with its cluster of small craft, nestles into a shallow cove. Multiplied many times over, the sight reproduces the activity of riverside Lewes in Medieval times and, indeed, up to the coming of the railways in the 19th century.

Returning back along South Street to the foot of Chapel Hill, brings one to the foot of the road of the Ancient Britons which ran from the Ouse ford

Cliffe High Street looking towards Cliffe Hill and the Cuilfail Estate.

over Caburn Hill to Glynde and the west. It is a very steep climb but well worth the effort for the magnificent view of the town to be gained from the top which is now part of Lewes Golf Club.

Looking north along the Ouse towards Lewes. The Lewes Boating Club is in the centre of the picture.

North of the town, to the right of the view from here, is the slope up onto the Downs from Offham Church whose spire is clearly visible in the trees at the foot of the hill. The line of the hill runs south over two chalk-pits gashed into its side and rises, finally, behind the town to the old race-course buildings high on the horizon. The Downs slope down from here to the western edge of the town, marked now by the prison buildings, the Neville Estate and the Victoria Hospital.

All this sweep of Downland is the site of the Battle of Lewes.

The Battle of Lewes

It might be considered poetic justice that the power and autocracy of the Normans was won on the Sussex battlefield of Senlac in 1066, only to crumble into the beginnings of defeat twenty miles away across the Weald at Lewes, two years short of two hundred years later.

Here the amalgam of Ancient Briton, Saxon and Norman finally began to coagulate into that fine blend of national spirit we know as English. The English, as a nation, can be said to have been born at Lewes in 1264.

At Lewes the spark was set to the trail that flowered into the nation that found its initial identity in the Hundred Years War of the 14th century and then in that burst of literary genius, second to none, of the Tudor period. From thence onwards it flowered into a democracy which evolved a parliamentary government unique in the World.

The blood of the Normans had thinned considerably by the beginning of the 13th century when Henry III, as a boy of nine, was crowned king after the disastrous reign of his father King John. Henry was no iron overlord. His chief loves were building, the Church and a life with a penchant for all things French. Finally, thirty years of squandered taxes and tithes brought opposition to a head. The barons, with memories of their initial victory of Magna Carta over Henry's father, only needed a leader to organise their protests. They found him in Simon de Montfort, a knight of high standing, and married to the King's sister, and of personal charisma.

Simon de Montfort appealed not only to the dissatisfied faction of the barons but to the lower orders such as the students of Oxford and the, always very influential, citizens of London. In other words, to the intelligentsia and the merchant classes.

The King resorted to arms and marched through the Norman Rapes of the South-east gathering support. Knowing he could count on religious support, he turned towards the powerful Priory of St. Pancras at Lewes, itself a county capital town with a strong castle held by the loyal seventh Lord John de Warenne.

He arrived right in the middle of the largest feast-day of the year celebrated at Lewes, the Feast of St. Pancras. The town was packed, the Priory also. Henry's descent on both, with a huge army, could have been less than welcome. But

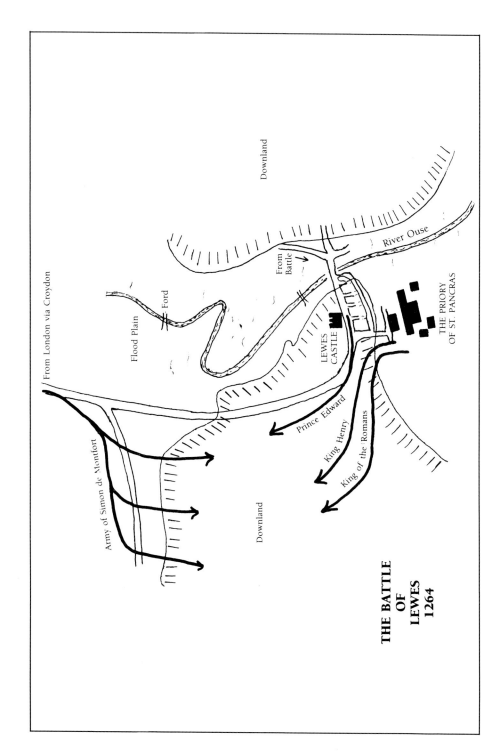

Downland

River Ouse

From London via Croydon

From Battle

THE PRIORY
OF ST. PANCRAS

Ford

Flood Plain

LEWES
CASTLE

Prince Edward

King Henry

King of the Romans

Army of Simon de Montfort

Downland

**THE BATTLE
OF
LEWES
1264**

somehow, room seems to have been found for them in the Priory, in the castle and around the town.

Simon was approaching from London via his own manor of Sheffield, now Sheffield Park, at Fletching. The Londoners had supported him to a man. They had marched for several days the long forty mile stretch and were only too glad to rest and regroup and take stock in the safety of Sheffield Manor and the village of Fletching.

Both the King and Simon de Montfort were nearing sixty and neither of them was thirsting for battle. Simon sent two bishops as messengers down to the Priory at Lewes seeking a peaceful settlement. But with the King was his twenty-seven year old, very energetic, eldest son, Edward and Henry's brother, Richard styled King of the Romans, an ambitious and impulsive character. Henry was persuaded to decline the olive branch. Battle was inevitable.

At first light on the day following, the 14th of May 1264, Simon marched his whole army to the foot of Offham Hill. The troops fanned out along the road to Ditchling for the climb up the escarpment of the Downs. The King's army seems to have been very dilatory, perhaps they were suffering the effects of celebrating the Priory's Feast too well. Simon's troops appeared over the crest of the hill in the morning sunlight and took the King's army completely by surprise.

He then advanced down the Racecourse hill. His standard and the less professionally trained of his troops came over the chalk-pits and behind what is now the Neville Estate. A hastily gathered army flooded up from the Priory and the castle. Battle was joined. Prince Edward, on the northern wing of the advance, since he had been stationed in the castle, made for the standard of the enemy and carved triumphantly through its guardians. Most of them were the unfortunate Londoners. After much slaughter, he hunted down the survivors, driving them off the hill and across the plain and back the way they had marched earlier. Few of them escaped.

Simon de Montfort meanwhile, had been even more successful in his battle with the Prince's father and uncle. The tide of battle, in this quarter, rolled remorselessly down to the town and down to the Priory, while the townsfolk cowered fearfully in their frantically barred houses and hovels.

The King's brother tried to take refuge in a windmill, standing west of the town wall beyond the church of St. Anne.

All the windmills that ringed Lewes from the 12th until the 19th century have now disappeared. An unusual relic of one, built by public subscription in 1806, is not far from this spot, up Pipe Passage. Here, there is a quaint round house built in brick and flint on the base of the demolished windmill.

The St. Anne's mill, made of wood, was little defence against de Montfort's soldiers. "Come out", they cried and promptly took him prisoner. With his brother a hostage and his army in total disarray, King Henry sought sanctuary himself in the Priory and surrendered.

The young Prince Edward, returning hopefully trimphant from his long chase across the Low Weald, was far too late. The battle was over and he and his father had been defeated.

The Mise of Lewes

The King delegated two representatives from the Priory to sue for terms. De Montfort chose two friars from the Friary.* He dictated his settlement, the Mise of Lewes. From this came the Parliament of 1265 when, for the first time ever, not only bishops and barons were called to attend the ruling of the Country, but also two knights from the shires and two burgesses from each of the boroughs favouring de Montfort's cause.

From this time, endorsed in the Model Parliament of the following reign, Lewes sent two burgesses to represent it at the Parliament in Westminster until a redistribution of representative procedures was brought in, by act of Parliament in 1867.

One wonders if, at the time, the townsfolk of Lewes really felt it had all been worth it. Their houses plundered, their town half ruined and many of their numbers killed or maimed for life in the savagery. Monks and friars tended the wounded as best they could and helped to bury the dead. How many dead there were is not exactly known. But in 1810, the ground was dug into just in front of the present prison gateway for remaking the old Lewes-Brighton coach road. Three large pits of human bones were discovered, estimated at around 1,500 men. A sad relic of the great battle.

Many more, no doubt, lie buried over a wide area along and across the rivers Ouse and Winterbourne and over the Downland. Some were reported to have been drowned in their flight or held by the swamps and mud until they were butchered. In 1769 the building of the new turnpike road at Offham turned up many more human remains thought to be those of the unfortunate Londoners fleeing before Prince Edward's cavalry.

The town and the Priory took a long time to recover their prosperity. A murage grant for three years, was made to help with the repairing of the town walls and buildings. This was the toll of one penny on every cart-load of iron passing through the gates and: "for every cart-load of iron for sale through the week, a halfpenny." In the next century, 1334, when there was the threat of French invasions, the town was again granted licence to levy customs for "inclosing the town".

Today Lewes commemorates the leaders of both sides of the battle. King Henry's Road and Prince Edward's Road lie adjoining each other on the Wallands Estate, cheek by jowl with Gundrada and her illustrious husband. De Montfort Road lies safely across the other side of the coombe up which runs The Avenue.

* *The Franciscan Friary of the Freres Minor, settled near the East Gate in 1241.*

Richard, the so-called "King of the Romans", they have firmly ignored. Perhaps the windmill he took refuge in remained to his memory until it was demolished. There have also been, at different times, three White Lion Inns in Lewes. The white lion was the armorial bearing of Simon de Montfort. The last of their signs can be seen raised almost triumphantly high along the huge wall below the castle in Westgate Street.

The Prince Edward, when he became king, as Edward I, revisited Lewes on at least six occasions, when he was entertained royally at the Priory. By then he had firmly grasped the reigns of power and recognised the worth of such boroughs as Lewes as being useful, and indeed necessary, jewels in his crown.

As to the battlefield, dealing with it as an historic site in its usual, practical way, the town eventually turned the highest part of it into a racecourse. The grandstands and stables still stand but not as a memorial to the great battle. It was left, appropriately, to the former, much respected Member of Parliament for Lewes, Sir Tufton Beamish, to raise the de Montfort memorial among the Priory ruins in 1964 when Lewes celebrated the seven-hundredth anniversary of the battle.

On the huge bronze helmet of the memorial are inscribed these words from "The Song of Lewes":

> "Now Englishmen, read on about that battle
> fought at Lewes' walls.
> Because of this you are alive and safe.
> Rejoice then in God . . . .
> Law is like fire, for it lights as truth
> warms as charity, burns as zeal.
> With these virtues as his guides, the King
> will rule well."

How Edward I would have appreciated that!

V. LEWES IN THE LATER MIDDLE AGES (1300-1500)

The next two centuries, 1300-1500, were years of wavering fortunes not only in the town but for all England. The 14th century was much occupied by the Hundred Years War with France. The 15th century continued the war into the civil war known as the Wars of the Roses.

But underneath all this clash of arms, in the villages and in the growing towns such as Lewes, great changes were taking place. In 1300 England was a country ruled by the upper classes, speaking in French, and clerics speaking Latin and commanded by Rome. Her rural peasants, still under the Feudal System, were slaves in all but name, bonded to the land of their lord. Their families, their time, their absolute allegiance, were all his, while on high, the last vestiges of the Age of Chivalry floated over the banners of the high-born knights and nobles.

By 1500 slavery had disappeared. The English language was being spoken by all and being printed and distributed countrywide. Towns were grasping at self-government with hands that knew well the feel of good, solid coin. The Age of Chivalry had disappeared into song and legend. The development of Lewes is the epitome of these great changes. In her case it was heralded, in 1347, by the final end of the line of the de Warenne dynasty.

The eighth earl, John, Earl of Sussex and Surrey, had married Joan, a grand-daughter of Edward I. But the match was not a happy one. History does not tell us whether he left her languishing in Lewes while he went off and found a lady more to his fancy in Maud, the daughter of a Norfolk knight from near his Norfolk holding of Castle Acre. By her he had several children but none legitimately by Joan. Even excommunication does not seem to have cooled his ardour, though he was obviously welcomed back into the religious fold at his death for he was buried, with all proper ceremony, in Lewes Priory in 1347 at the ripe age of sixty-one.

There passed the last of the de Warennes. Lordship of the castle was

"Men avoided the twittens at night". A typical Lewes twitten. This one leads from St. Anne's Hill to Rotten Row.

inherited by his nephew, the Earl of Arundel, who saw it as a possession but not as a home. At last the castle stood untenanted. Its keep and barbican might still dominate the town in stone, but not in spirit. The long bondage was over.

The townsfolk reacted swiftly to their new-found freedom. At the first local rising in 1381, they broke into the castle and removed as much stone as they could lay their hands on for their own use. It is also said that they freely helped themselves to his lordship's wine! It was a sign of the times. The whole country was in a state of upheaval as a result of the drastic changes brought about by the ravages of the Black Death.

The Black Death

We cannot, in this age of hygiene and medicine, conceive of the awful horror of the plagues of the Middle Ages. There had been smaller, intermittent outbreaks of them ever since man began to travel, but the Black Death of 1348 was an altogether more devastating visitation.

It was an horrific catastrophe, a murdering wave that swept through town and village alike. Nowhere escaped. It scourged the countryside from the summer of 1348 until the winter of 1349, recurring at intervals afterwards, particularly in the insanitary townships of the day, until its final appearance, centuries later in 1665 as the Great Plague, under Charles II.

In the two years of its first ferocious onslaught, 1348-9, it left nearly two million people dead. Nearly half the estimated population of the country. Whole villages ceased to exist, everybody having died. Hamsey, just north of Lewes, is thought to have been decimated in this way. Heighton in Firle Park also disappeared. In Battle half the monks and the Abbot perished. Eight out of thirteen of the priory of Michelham died, and in Lewes, the Prior and the Sub-Prior died and the foundation never fully recovered from the disaster.

In Lewes we have no record of the number of deaths, we can only imagine the horror of those months of suffering and despair. Men avoided the twittens, especially at night, when one could stumble over a corpse in the darkness and be condemned without reprieve. The friars and monks toiled bravely to bring what comfort and medicines might alleviate the suffering, if not cure. The hospital of the Priory was virtually the only medical centre of the town. Possibly this is why, at that time, the Priory built the new hospital for the town outside its gates in Southover.

A hospital so built would have consisted of a long hall, like the nave of a church, with a chapel at one end. At the other end were sited the kitchen etc. The chapel of this hospital of St. James can still be seen in Southover Street just across the road from the Grange. It is a little known, untouched gem, of fourteenth century architecture.

War, pestilence and panic ordinances produced by a weak government in 1381, erupted into revolution in the South-east as the Peasants' Revolt. With only half the number of the work-force available, after the Black Death, the peasant workers began to realise their worth. They marched on the centres of authority. In Lewes they attacked and damaged the castle.

In the next century, in 1450, the rebellion led by Jack Cade in Kent, was again supported by the town, this time to a man. The list of those who were granted pardons after that event included: The burgesses, the two constables, many named individuals of All Saints parish, Cliffe and Westout (St. Anne's) and Southover. Finally it included the Prior of Lewes himself and all his community! Lewes was finding her strength and her independence in no uncertain way.

The People of Lewes

We have by this time, details in a number of written documents, of many of the leading Medieval citizens of the town. Some of their names are still familiar to us today. There was Philip Walwer and William Walwer. The latter was M.P. for Lewes in 1319 and again in 1324. Walwers Lane is named after him, the twitten running down from School Hill to Friars Walk.

There was also the Brooman family who lived here in the same century and are commemorated by Brooman Lane in the area.

Philip Walwer, interestingly, received some property on condition that he never sold it on to a religious house or to a Jew! Agnes Pinwell, who lived in Pinwell Street which is now Church Lane, was not so barred and did endow the Priory. The well of "Pinwell" was a spring in the grounds of the Friary now to be found as a drinking well on the opposite side of Friars Walk where it was erected in Victorian times. Along side it is a relic of the Friary building, a carved archway saved from the demolished Friary which was closed at the Dissolution of the Monasteries.

Robert Spicer was another Lewes merchant of standing. He lived near, or on, the site of the present Town Hall and was M.P. for Lewes in 1322 and 1323. Near here too must have dwelt John Aylward who died in 1544, for the present War Memorial site, at the top of School Hill, was known as Aylwards Corner until very recent times.

It was these men and others of the town who slowly heaved the constitution out of its old manorial status to the new, more independent and self-governing condition that took Lewes into the Tudor period.

We have to wait until 1542 to read in the first available Town Book our first clear details of this. By this time these wealthier merchants, living in their tall, timber-framed houses the length of the High Street, had already provided for an established, elected body of "Twelve" to control the town's affairs. The actual number of the "Twelve" varied from twelve to eighteen and they were chosen from a society of twenty-four worthy men associated with them in governing.

From the "Twelve" were chosen the over-all officials, the two Constables and the two "Boroughs". The Borough Court was still held on the first Monday after Michelmas. It is interesting to note the particular duties of the officials who

Drinking fountain in Friar's Walk built in 1874 to commemorate the ancient Pinwell spring which originally stood in the Friary grounds opposite.

were appointed: Clerks of the Corn Market, the Fish-market and the Butchery, the Ale-tasters, the Scavenger and the Sealer of Leather.

These were annual appointments. That of the "Twelve" were often for active life, and election, when called for, was at the great Whitsun festival, the biggest fair of the year.

This, and the fair held on St. Pancras Day, were times of great festivity in Lewes and a centre for celebration for all the surrounding countryside. For Lewes still was essentially a product of the Downland and Wealden area in which she lay. Men of the town still owned property in the surrounding countryside and had an intimate interest in the farming of it. Others outside owned property in the town, led by the Archbishop of Canterbury from his estate in Malling, the Prior of St. Pancras and the Bishop of Chichester.

Above all, as in the Cotswold country and parts of East Anglia, wool had become the staple product of the country and the wealth of Lewes grew with the wealth of the wool trade since she was the collecting centre and the port for a rich wool producing region.

It has been suggested that the name Ranscombe, south-east of Southerham, is a variation of Rams Coombe, i.e. where the rams were sheltered in winter. Whereas, at the other side of Caburn Hill, Earwig Corner may signify the holding where the ewes were folded, "wick" or "wig" coming from the Saxon word for a farm.

The Wars of the Roses, following on after the seemingly unending Hundred Years War with France, also gave a healthy impetus to the Wealden iron industry. Lewes was the chief trading centre and port for this too and gained accordingly. Indeed, when trade with France was resumed in the mid-15th century, at the end of the Hundred Years War, Lewes was one of the comparatively few towns who continued to grow steadily in prosperity as compared to towns in the East, the West and the Midlands, many of which had suffered sadly from the Civil Wars of the Roses (1450-1485).

The Church in the Medieval Age

It had suited the Norman conquerors to support the power of the Church. They had invaded with the blessing of Rome from the first. The Norman approach to religion was essentially practical and businesslike. To raise magnificent properties, such as that of St. Pancras, to the honour of God, was the current form of insurance policy, more often than not, against an after life of purgatory for a guiltily brutal life on this earth.

Furthermore, honour so bought for God and the Church was naturally earthly honour for the builder in the estimation of his peers and underlings.

In Lewes, most of the present town churches were built, and added to, throughout these years. At one time, before the old Saxon chapels were swept away, there were ten churches or chapels within the walls of the town and four outside. It would seem a high number, even then, for a town with a possible population of around two thousand people. Those closed and demolished in Medieval times included St. Martin's, St. Andrew's, St. Mary-in-foro, St. Peter the less, St. Nicholas-in-foro, St. Sepulchre and Holy Trinity. Outside the walls St. Peter, in Westout, was also closed.

Today there are six churches for a population ten times larger, only five of which are in religious use. Added to which is one Roman Catholic church and a number of chapels. Of these, the church of St. John-sub-Castro is the oldest foundation. It was rebuilt on its Saxon foundations but little of the Medieval structure is extant as it was again rebuilt, in Victorian times, on a new base in 1839. Its Saxon remains have already been described.

The church of St. Michael, by the Westgate, still keeps its Norman or Early English round flint tower, perhaps a lighted beacon for travellers in those days. The knapped flint wall that abuts the High Street is 18th century (1748), the nave is 13th century and the south arcade dates from the 14th century. The west tower is 15th century as also are the two fine brasses within. There is also the tomb of Sir Nicholas Pelham of the 16th century. His plaque represents him still kneeling, with his lady wife and all the respectful progeny of their ten children kneeling alongside. The austere street-fronted building hides a tree-shaded churchyard, green and surprisingly peaceful in the centre of such a busy town, climbing to the foot of the towering castle motte behind.

The church of St. John the Baptist, as has been mentioned already, dates from the 12th century. It contains much Norman stonework still in good order. The chancel was added by the Victorians in 1884, also the small chapel, in Norman style, to hold the recently unearthed relics of the Priory founders in 1847. Their black marble tomb-cover originally covered the Lady Gundrada's tomb in the Priory and is inscribed with the date of her death (1085) and her virtues.

Now held as the "mother" church for the town, the church of St. Anne, Westout, was also built outside the walls in the 12th century. It is indominitably Norman from its tiny (five foot eight inches high) rounded doorway to its solidly carved interior columns. The chancel was rebuilt in the 13th century, although the arch is modern. The font has fine 12th century carvings, the roof dates from 1538 and there is a splendid canopied tomb dating from the 14th century.

It seems incredible that a holy woman of the 12th century decided to give her whole existence to the service of her God and allowed herself to be walled up in a tiny cell here by the chancel wall. Day after day she lived out her life and, when she died, her little cold cell became her coffin as it remains today. What magic was there about Lewes, and the faith to be found there, in those days long ago to inspire such sacrifice? And that of that other anchorite, Prince Magnus in St. John-sub-Castro? Perhaps the same that gave seventeen local men and women, four hundred years later, the courage to face being burned alive rather than recant one jot of their firm religious faith.

St. Thomas's Church in the Cliffe was, like St. Michael's Church, thought to have been founded by the Canons of Malling. Built in honour of the martyred Archbishop in the late 12th century, it was added to in the three succeeding centuries. There is a fine carved squint in the south aisle and an interesting copy of the charter granted to the Cliffe in 1409 by Henry IV enabling it to hold a market, in the High Street, and two annual fairs, in the Fairplace behind the church, on the feasts of St. Matthew and St. Mark.

There is also a rare painted model of the Tudor Royal Arms hanging in the south aisle and a hatchment of King George I.

Only the 16th century tower remains of the last of the town churches to date from this period, All Saint's Church. The rest of the church was rebuilt in 1806 and 1883. Inside there is a monument to the grandfather of John Evelyn, the 17th century diarist, and also the two stone figures of children which stood outside the first National School of Lewes sited at the bottom of Station Street. The church is now an Arts Centre.

Although additions to the two town churches still appear to have continued through the 15th century, the power of the Roman Catholic Church, in England, was at last steadily on the wane.

However, while the power of the ecclesiastics declined, the power of the great barons swelled to fill the vacancy to such an extreme that civil war inevitably ensued. Fighting began in 1455. Fortunately for Lewes, while most of England was involved in the fighting in this War of the Roses, she lay quiet and comparatively safe behind the bulwark of the Wealden Forest.

In the seeds of the dispute, in 1399, when Henry Bolinbroke was advancing his initial claim to the throne as Henry IV, nearby Pevensey was the occasion for a local involvement in the faction fighting. From here we have "the oldest letter in the English language". The writer was Joan, the stalwart wife of Sir John Pelham, Lord of the castle, who was manfully holding the castle against siege by King Richard's supporters.

"My dear Lord," she writes. "If it like you to know my fare, I am here laid by in manner of siege with the County of Sussex, Surrey and a great parcel of Kent. So that I may not go out nor no victuals get in . . .
Your own poor J.Pelham."

It is good to know that she was rescued by her husband who was richly rewarded for his support by the new dynasty of the Lancastrians.

Lewes, with no resident member of the aristocracy, kept her gates, her ears and her eyes shut against the clash of arms. The old baronage in the rest of the country succeeded in killing off the major part of itself in the thirty years of civil war that lasted from 1455 to 1485. When the new Tudor age dawned with the succession of Henry VII in 1485, the demise of the old noble houses had left room for a new class of minor nobles to match and support the new royal house.

VI. TUDOR LEWES

The "new men" of Tudor times had risen slowly to positions of growing prestige over the 14th and 15th centuries as their personal fortunes had increased by trade, by judicial successes, by shrewd financial investments and even shrewder marriages.

In their rich doublets and hose and flaunting long trains of attendants, they were to be the new Gentry of Tudor England. In East Sussex, chief among them were the Sackvilles, the Pelhams of Laughton, the Gorings of Danny, the Gages of Firle and the Morleys of Glynde. It is a sign of the importance of Lewes that many of them felt called to build a town residence here to add to their country seat or seats and to their, later, London residences.

The Pelhams had been typical knights of the Medieval times earning the famous "buckle" on the field of Poitiers in 1356. Lands in Sussex came to them when they backed the winning side and helped Henry Bolinbroke to the throne of England as Henry IV. Their first family stronghold near Lewes was at Laughton. The red-brick tower of their house still rises like a square lighthouse out of the flat, wealden plain, the Pelham buckle carved on each wall. It was a damp and ill-drained place however and the family deserted it later for the healthier site of Halland Park where, when the current Pelham was eventually made Duke of Newcastle, the returning family coach was greeted with peals of bells from every local village church en-route.

Sir Nicholas Pelham married a Sackville and has a fine family wall monument in St. Michael's Church in Lewes to commemorate his martial feat in protecting Lewes from the French attack at Seaford in 1545. He was the first Pelham to have a house in the town. This was on the site of the present White Hart Hotel, in the very centre of the town, in 1568. The 19th century frontage of the present hotel hides the original Elizabethan interior. The back premises and the kitchen show the best preserved remains of the original Pelham house.

George Goring bought his house, in St. Andrew's Lane, in 1563, from the heir of John Comot, Constable for the town in 1540. St. Andrew's Lane was then a busy town street, including in its buildings a cider-makers and a slaughter-house since it was so near to the market in the High Street.

George Goring was already a figure of local importance. He became Sheriff of Sussex and Surrey in 1572 and had stood as M.P. for Lewes since 1562. Pulling down the old Medieval structure in 1579, he raised a magnificent Elizabethan dwelling in its place which still stands today. It cost him £2,000 which was a fortune at that time. Not surprising perhaps that he died, in 1594, owing the Crown nearly £20,000! However, his heirs inherited the mansion. Unfortunately they took the losing, Royalist, side in the 17th century Civil War and so were forced to sell their Lewes house to a Parliamentarian who resold it to Sir Thomas Pelham in 1654.

The Pelhams then lived in it, as their town house, renaming it "Pelham House", for the next century and a half. During this time, they re-fronted the Elizabethan facade in the more stylish Classic pattern of the 18th century in 1790 and 1812. The house still contains inside the superb panelling and carving of the Elizabethan craftsmen now carefully preserved by East Sussex County Council which acquired it in 1928.

George Goring's brother, Sir Henry, built his town house where the Westgate Chapel now stands with the Bull Inn next door to it. The Westgate Chapel looks quite insignificant when viewed from the High Street. However, viewing from the east side, in Stewards Inn Lane, gives an entirely different impression. In the wall above can be seen the fine mullioned window set in the original flint wall of the old Elizabethan mansion with below, an original Tudor doorway.

The Bull Inn was the original Bull hostelry that stood, in Medieval times, just inside the Westgate of the town. The building* that now stands there was the northern part of the building. The southern portion was pulled down by Sir Henry Goring when he replaced it with the imposing flint and stone house which, like Pelham House, commanded wide views of the Ouse valley from its south-facing garden.

Between 1698 and 1700 it was converted into the chapel which it remains to this day.

It is interesting to note that in the deeds of the property, Sir Henry is detailed as having bought the original inn, in 1583, from "Thomas Matthew, Yeoman of Lewes". The yeomen, again, were another rising class of the Tudor age. The Matthews were a stalwart family of standing in the town. Thomas was Constable in 1560 and Chief Constable in 1570. His brothers, three in all, lived nearby in the High Street and owned a number of town properties.

The yeoman was technically one possessing land to the value of forty shillings and was qualified to serve on juries and assist in minor elections. Just outside Lewes, in the hamlet of Hamsey, an excellent idea of their status, and a good example of the house they could afford to live in, stands as the house still called "Yeomans".

George Morley of Glynde was another of the new generation of minor noblemen who settled not in, in this case, but near to Lewes. He was the son of an iron-founder whose fortunes had risen swiftly with the developing Wealden iron industry in the 15th and 16th centuries. He built a fine Tudor mansion, Glynde Place, three miles east of Lewes at the same time as the Gages were marrying into land and wealth and came from near Cirencester to build Firle Place just under Firle Beacon south of Lewes.

The Morleys and the Gages are two sides of the religious changes of the Tudor age. The Morleys became sturdy Protestants while the Gage family adhered to the old Roman faith and paid heavily for it in fines during Elizabethan times.

* Bull House, now the offices of the Sussex Archaeological Society.

The new nobility held sway over much of the countryside. It is heartening to read in the old documents how much the lesser, untitled towns-folk also felt their local responsibilities.

We read that Thomas Matthew, with three friends of like standing, paid to have one of the bells of St. Michael's church recast. Then there was, in 1565, a Mrs Holter, the widow of the town Constable for 1547, who gave ten pounds towards building the new Market House. Chalices, patons and flagons were continually being presented to the various town churches and the oak pulpit given by Herbert Springett in 1620 is still to be seen in the church of St. Anne.

Before the dissolution of the Priory, no doubt most of the gifts would have been directed there. With the liberating of religious ideas came the greater, civic, loyalty to the growing town. In 1611 Thomas Blunt, barber-surgeon, gave the town its silver-gilt cup. His tomb is still to be seen at the entrance to St. John-sub-Castro's churchyard. Such is the high place of honour he is held in the town that, even as late as Victorian times, resolutions were being made to restore his tomb to a proper condition commensurate with the respect still due to his name.

Sir Thomas Springett of Ringmer, who had a house in Lewes, left £100 "out of his love to the said town and townsmen . . . and in regard of his birth and education at Lewes where (his) father, Herbert Springett Esq., always dwelt". John Rowe, another Lewes worthy, gave to the town "The town Brooks", now part of the Pells. Best of all perhaps, was the gift of Mrs Agnes Morley, for she it was who founded and endowed the Lewes Free Grammar School in 1512.

Education had been provided by the Priory up to its closure, but this school was virtually a non-ecclesiastical establishment and a product, not only of civic generosity, but also of the widespread growing thirst for learning. The school was founded in Eastport Lane, Southover. It was moved to St. Anne's Hill in 1714 and rebuilt in 1815 in fitting Tudor style at the foot of St. Anne's Hill where it remains to this day.

The Streets and Buildings of Tudor Lewes

Tudor Lewes was thus a flourishing, bustling town, the centre of a productive hinterland, and much enhanced by the new property being built by the "nouveau riches". So much of it has been refaced or rebuilt since, that it is not so easy to visualise it immediately from a walk through the centre of the town. Pipe Passage and Pope's Entry both give a glimpse of the past and the inset "Castle Antiques" presents a picture of fine timbered housing nestling against the bulk of the castle keep.

Diverting through Pope's Entry and turning right along Castle Ditch, reveals another little treasure of Tudor Lewes, a moulded stone doorway set into the bank of the ditch. Formerly it led through to the stables that served the High Street houses, now it serves a lonely life leading to nothing but a brick wall.

Bricks were now at a premium in the new, brick-building Tudor Age. So many were in demand that brick-works sprang up all round the clay-based Weald.

Barbican House, now the headquarters of the Sussex Archaeological Society, is a Tudor house re-fronted in the 18th century, as are also numbers 174 and 175 in the High Street. Across the road, numbers 66 to 74 are nearly all basically Medieval or Tudor. Number 72 still has the original undercroft cellar. West of Keere Street, numbers 99 to 103 are all similarly 16th century in origin.

In the other direction, School Hill, as a name, dates back to 1498. Just before the top of the hill, where the Town Hall now stands, was the Star Inn standing on the corner of Star Lane, now renamed Fisher Street. The name Star Lane was preserved until recently, on the wall-board of Beard's Brewery on the old brewery wall. The Star was the largest of the many town inns. At this time it may have looked very much as the famous Star Inn at Alfriston looks today.

Across the river, at the foot of the hill, some of the buildings on the north side of the Cliffe retain original timber framing and jetties. The south side was almost entirely rebuilt, as far east as Morris Road, when the road was widened in the nineteenth century.

At the foot of Cliffe Hill is a modest late Tudor building on the corner of Chapel Hill. Indeed, looking up the winding lane from the west side of South Street, one can picture clearly how it must have looked in Tudor times. On the right is the timbered frontage just mentioned, while on the left is the mounting row of cottages (now brick-faced) of the same age. This little lane wound up over Cliffe Hill, skirting Caburn to the village of Glynde. It was the road, or bostal, of the Ancient Britons.

But the pride of the town is historic Keere Street, so named since at least 1272. This was the old lane, just outside the westgate in Medieval times, that ran down to the Winterbourne by the side of the town wall.

At the top of the street is an unspoilt 15th century building with a milestone now fixed into the wall, moved from the opposite side of the road, recording the distance of 50 miles from the Standard in Cornhill, 49 miles to Westminster Bridge, and 8 miles to Brighthelmston. The building, a bookshop, rises to three storeys of magnificent timber-framing with the picturesque overhung jetties of Tudor architecture.

Keere Street keeps its old blue-cobbled surface of the Medieval Era and is famous, traditionally, as the street down which, in the 18th century, the Prince of Wales, later George IV, drove his coach and four. He was driving from the race-meeting on Lewes Racecourse to dine at the Grange at the foot of the street. One can only hope that the legend has become enlarged with age for the drive would have been merciless to the horses. In fact, a local paper of 1799 reports that the prince actually drove on through the town to the top of School Hill where he "dismounted and led his mount to the bottom".

A more verified story about Keere Street is to be found in the town book for

The timbered 15th century Bookshop at the junction of Keere Street and the High Street.

1774 where the road is called "Care Hill" or "Scare Hill". A guinea was paid to an intrepid citizen for "watching the small-pox on Scare Hill" and a shilling for "gin to wash James Kent of the small-pox". A bravely earned guinea!

In Southover too, timber-framed houses dating from the Tudor Age are still preserved for our delight. Anne of Cleves House is a large, picturesque building, along Southover High Street, of oak-framing with part brick and flint infilling. The roofs are covered in old, hand-made tiles and large slabs of Horsham stone. It is very doubtful that the ex-Queen Anne actually lived here at any time. The Manor of Southover was given to her, among many others, on her amicable divorce from Henry VIII. The cellars are part 14th century and also contain stone from the dissolved Lewes Priory.

The ancient road, still part-cobbled, following the original western defence wall of the town from the Westgate to the Winterbourne. The wall, restored through the centuries, can still be seen behind the houses on the east side of the street.

Across the adjoining Potters Lane is a group of early 16th century cottages equally well preserved, with Tudor arched doorways and timbered upper storeys. Anne of Cleves House is now a museum of the Sussex Archaeological Society, rich in local history.

Retracing eastwards along the street, the plot at the corner of St. James' Street was the former local pound for stray animals. Behind it was the local wheelwright's shop.

The Reformation in Lewes

Southover grew up around the gateway to the great St. Pancras Priory which, by 1538, had stood as a symbol of the Church in all its power for four hundred and fifty years.

The fall of its columns and towers, on November 16th 1537, marked conclusively the end of the old and the beginning of the new in the history of Lewes. The people of the town and of the surrounding county had had a century of peace, while the Wars of the Roses waged elsewhere, to become very much aware of the "New Thinking" that was spreading across from the Continent.

Since the days of Wycliffe, his followers, the Lollards, had been spreading the words of the Bible, now translated into English, and their interpretations of them, particularly through south and south-east England. Sussex was already familiar with roadside preaching, the Franciscan Order having established their small friary at the foot of the hill, in Lewes, between the walls and the river in 1241. This had been an outgoing order who spread their teaching far and wide through the towns and villages. It is significant that two of these Grey Friars represented the Barons' side, against two of the Priory monks representing the King's party, in agreeing the "Mise of Lewes" after the Battle of Lewes.

Lewes had had first hand experience of the enormous wealth and power of the Church. The St. Pancras Priory owned a fifth of all the countryside in addition to property in the town itself. The neighbouring Abbey at Battle contrôlled as much again, if not more. Moreover, in this age when national feeling was still a heady novelty, these were essentially foreign foundations, established by Frenchmen and powered by Rome.

For England it was fortuitous that, at this critical time of change in her history, she should have been blessed with a ruling dynasty, the Tudors, whose strength of character and reigning ability were so outstanding.

The first of the line, Henry VII, ruled with no standing army captained by over-powerful lords. He, and his successors, governed through the local gentry in their shires, the Justices of the Peace. The office had been originated in the late 12th century and had increased in importance from then on.

These local Justices of the Peace, in Tudor times, were the same New Gentry we have seen settling themselves in and around Lewes in their town houses and large country mansions. Cases from the shire at large were heard by them at the Courts of Quarter Sessions. More local parish matters were considered at the Courts of Petty Sessions.

Fast rising standards of education in locally established schools, colleges and in the Inns of Court made them very efficient in such administration. Many of them, and their descendants, became the famous lawyers of the next two centuries. The most notable of these Tudor and Elizabethan lawyers of Lewes was John Rowe, Steward of the Barony of Lewes and Chief Constable in 1598. He became a principal of Cliffords Inn in London. His sons also became Fellows of the same Inn.

But at the heart of the new age of learning was the Bible. By the later 16th and 17th centuries the Bible had become so much a part of their everyday thoughts and speech that the English were known to the people of their day as the "People of the Book". In 1538 a new translation of the Bible, based on Tyndale's work, was placed in every church in Lewes as they were throughout the country.

Two years before this, the "Reformation Parliament" of 1536 had called for the closing of the 375 lesser monasteries and abbeys. Bayham Abbey, in the north of Sussex, had already been dissolved by Wolsey in 1525. Here the local people protested angrily and actually reinstated the abbot for a time.

When it came to the turn of the larger foundations of Sussex, there was no such public protest. The townsfolk of Lewes watched the destruction of their Priory silently and then, as unemotionally, moved in to salvage what they could for their own use. The Prior and monks of Sussex, it should be here mentioned, were not turned out to starve as is sometimes claimed. They were given pensions and local benefices. The Abbot of Battle received an annual pension worth £10,000 of today's money. The Prior of Lewes, Robert Peterson, was given enough cathedral offices around England to keep him in comfort to the end of his days. The monks and friars from the dissolved friary, became parish priests. Some even, later married and settled down to family life.

The House of the Grey Friars was bought by John Kyne, M.P. for Lewes, in 1544 and rebuilt into a large Tudor house. By marriage it subsequently came to John Shurley, barrister, and one of the "Upper Ten" gentlemen of standing in Elizabethan Lewes. The Shurley family estate was at Isfield.

Thomas Cromwell was granted the dissolved Priory. In its destruction he had preserved the Prior's Lodgings to become a residence for his son John whom he had married to the late Queen Jane's sister. Falling from favour, like his predecessor Wolsey, Cromwell lost all his possessions, and his head, two years later. The Prior's house, in its thirty acres of garden, was known by then as The Lord's Place. At Cromwell's fall the Manor of Southover was given to Anne of Cleves. At her death, in 1557, it was acquired by the Sackvilles, viz. Lord Buckhurst, and the Earls of Dorset. Finally, the Lord's Place was destroyed by fire and never rebuilt.

In the reign of the third Tudor monarch, Edward VI, the break with Rome and the spread of Protestantism was completed. Services in all the churches of Lewes, as elsewhere, were now in English instead of in Latin, and all according to the new Book of Common Prayer. The chained Bible was read from every lectern.

The word of God was a precious study far and wide and nowhere more so than in Sussex. This, and the searing events of the following reign, set the seal on Sussex Protestantism, including that of Lewes, in its most sincere form, and laid the foundation for the further swing to non-conformity in the years to come.

The Lewes Martyrs

Queen Mary (1553-58), the last of the Tudors, made a final, determined attempt to restore the Catholic faith of her Spanish upbringing urged on by ambassadors from France and Spain. The persecution of those holding to the Protestant faith was merciless, especially in London and the south-east counties where the auto-de-fe tactics of Jesuit Spain resulted in nearly three hundred people being publicly burned to death rather than retract one tenet of their new-found convictions.

Sussex contributed thirty-six of these, between 1555 and 1557, seventeen of whom were martyred in the main street of Lewes.

June 22nd 1557 dawned in Lewes. Along the High Street, outside the present Town Hall, the stakes were set ready for ten men and women of Sussex to die for their faith.

The townsfolk had gathered from their stalls, their timbered houses and their crowded hovels down the twittens. More poured through the massive westgate and pushed their way to the huge pile of faggots and barrels surmounted by the ten ominous stakes. They surged up School Hill from the bridge over the river and more from across the Winterbourne.

The soldiers, shouting and threatening, tried to keep the crowds seemly, some on horseback from Firle Place, for Sir John Gage was in command of law and order for the Queen.

Down in the dark cellar of the Star Inn the ten martyrs, chained and dishevelled, shuffled up the stone steps to ground level and emerged, unkempt and dazzled, into the summer light. Leader of them was Richard Woodman of Warbleton, well known in the town. A wealthy

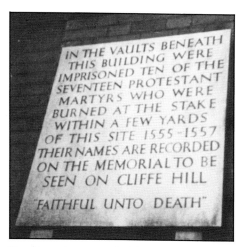

The Martyr's Memorial slab on the wall of the Lewes Town Hall. Placed by the Sussex Martyrs' Memorial Council in June 1949.

ironmaster of the Weald forest and respected church warden in his village of Warbleton, he left a wife and young children. With him was his friend, George Stevens from the same village.

Next came William Maynard, a gentleman from Mayfield. He had been arrested with his maid, Thomasina Wood. Also from Mayfield were Mary Groves and Anne Ashdon or Ashdowne, both wives with families. A John Ashdon or Ashdowne, also from Mayfield, is recorded as being martyred at Chichester.

After them were dragged Margery Morris and her son James, from Cade Street near Heathfield, and Alexander Hosman, a young yeoman of Rotherfield. Lastly there was Dennis Burges of Buxted.

One cannot think that Richard Woodman at least would have suffered being chained to the stake without making his presence felt. He had a ready tongue in defence of his faith and had bested his accusers, in the various prisons he had been held in, on over thirty occasions.

With the lighting of the faggots would have come the flaring of shouts of cheer from the crowd and exhortations and blessings from the victims. And then the crackling of the flames, the smoke billowing and the warning shouts of the soldiers to keep the crowd at bay. Screams and shouts and snatches of psalms and prayers until, mercifully, the flames completed their work and only the ashes were left. . . .

The courage and inspiration of the ten heroes and heroines of that fateful day still lives on. What we, in this age, take so lightly as our granted liberty in religion, was treason and heresy in 1557.

Four times altogether the tragic persuasion of Mary Tudor lit the martyrs' fires in Lewes. Two burnings had taken place in the June of the previous year, 1556, putting to death two men from Ardingly, two from Woodmancote and two from Hellingly. Prior to that, on July 22nd 1555, the first of the Sussex martyrs, the brewer Deryk Carver of Brighthelmstone was burned. He had been accused of "saying prayers in English" and of reading the Bible in English at his home in Black Lion Street. His house is now marked by a plaque bearing a sign of a burning fire.

In 1901 a memorial was raised to all the martyrs of Lewes at a cost of £900. The land for it was given by Mr Isaac Vinall who developed the Cuilfail Estate. It stands high on Cliffe Hill with the names of the seventeen martyrs carved on it. Typically for Lewes, it was erected by private sponsorship, and is maintained by the Sussex Martyrs Commemoration Council. They are also responsible for the plaque on the wall of the Town Hall which records the burnings and concludes with the words, "Faithful unto death".

The memorial on Cuilfail is well placed. As a view point it actually overlooks the very spot, at the top of School Hill, where the fires were lit. It is open to the public and can be reached on foot or by vehicle through the Cuilfail Estate. There is a smaller replica of it at Punnetts Town, near Heathfield, in the grounds of the Independent Chapel. This too surveys the countryside where the men and women of Sussex died so bravely.

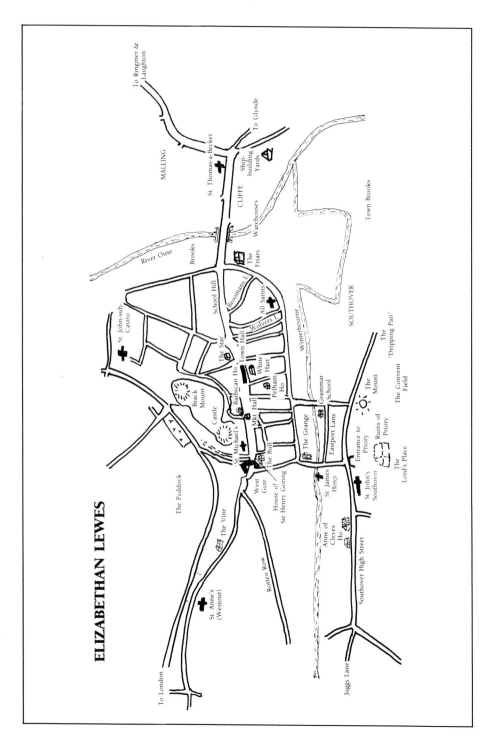

ELIZABETHAN LEWES

VII. ELIZABETHAN LEWES 1558-1603

What rejoicing there must have been in Lewes when the new Queen Elizabeth came to the throne with her young, alert mind and her passionate love for her England and her People. The bonfires blazed again, but this time in wholehearted celebration.

Bonfires from this time on would mean something very special to the people of Lewes.

The same capacity that the people of Elizabethan England had for facing the tragedies and hardships of their lives, gave them the optimism to enjoy the good times to the full. Their towns, picturesque as they seem to us now, were filthy and smelly. The streets were full of people and animals and rubbish, and their dwellings were dark, uncomfortable and draughty. Typhoid and plague were a constant threat and old-age began at thirty-five!

The wealthy traders and craftsmen lived in the most comfortable circumstances, but the poorer folk, renting their crowded lodgings, and the apprentices, bound to their masters, mainly lived a miserably cold and harsh life. Any cause for celebration and pageantry was seized on boisterously. Saints Days and market days were times when the drudgery of life could be flung aside. The wandering minstrels played, the people danced and shouted and sang and forgot their troubles, or drowned them in whatever brew their meagre savings could buy them in the ale-houses.

The larger ale-houses now became hosteleries. With lodging no longer being provided for travellers at the Priories and Abbeys, the country needed inns big enough to accommodate the visitors to its towns, and accommodation for their horses and carriages. In Lewes, the Bull Inn became one such, together with the Star Inn which was the largest in the town, and the Vine Inn outside the walls in Westout on St. Anne's Hill.

The Vine was already flourishing as an inn in 1577 when a successful brewer from Southover, Thomas Polland, bought it and rebuilt the frontage, dated it, and added his initials. He also added an imposing Tudor porch as well as modernising the interior. It later came into the hands of Henry Shelley (in 1663) and has been known as Shelleys ever since. The facing along the street was again updated, and a new garden front added, in the next century. It was extended and the garden redesigned with terrace, lawns and trees in the 19th century. It is now, again, a very lovely residential hotel.

But the finest of all Elizabethan houses in Lewes is to be found at the foot of Keere Street in the Winterbourne valley. In the original dwelling here lived the Agnes Morley who founded the Lewes Grammar School, appropriately enough only a few hundred yards from the former Girls Grammar School. In 1572 her house was bought by William Newton, who had high standing in the town as the Steward to the Earl of Dorset. He rebuilt it in stone from the

Southover Grange, built for Agnes Morley the founder of the Lewes Grammar School. It was rebuilt by William Newton in 1572 using stone from the remains of the Lewes Priory.

ruins of the priory, and particularly the remains of the Lord's Place which had been destroyed by fire in 1568.

Agnes Morley's house was now called Southover Grange. It still stands, a

Stonework from the ruined Priory of St. Pancras enhances the beauty of the Southover Grange Gardens.

beautiful Elizabethan building faced in Caen stone with stone-mullioned windows and the ornate chimney stacks of the period. Inside is an Elizabethan oak staircase, two of the original fireplaces from the Priory, and a Tudor fireplace carved with Newton's initials and the date 1572.

The gardens have been wonderfully preserved and enriched by the local council who now own the house for the use of the town. Archways and other stone relics from the old Priory enhance the view at every turn, while the tamed Winterbourne still flows steadily through the lawns and carpet beds of flowers. It is a remarkably beautiful garden and open to the public at all times.

William Newton had a daughter, Elizabeth, who married a Thomas Elphick from Seaford. His son, William Newton, married, as his second wife, the widow of John Stansfield of Cliffe and South Malling. John Stansfield had bought the Deanery of South Malling from the Earl of Dorset who had acquired it after the dissolution of the religious house there. Stones and flints of the original monks' buildings are still to be seen incorporated into the mellow outside brick walls of the Deanery.

John also contributed largely to the building and endowment of the present church at South Malling. He did not live to see it in use, for John Evelyn, the famous diarist, his grandson, tells us that he died in the year that the church was consecrated, 1627.

John Evelyn, as a young boy, had been sent out of London, where the plague was again raging, to the comparative safety of Lewes. He lived, after his grandfather's death, with his grandmother (remarried to William Newton) at the Grange, Southover. From here he attended the Grammar School in Eastport Lane and later studied at a school in the Cliffe.

With fine new stone and brick buildings and schools established, it is easy to see that prosperity was growing fast in Lewes through the late 16th century. With the break up of the huge Priory estates even more of the land in the vicinity of the town had come into the hands of the new gentry and yeomen farmers. They exploited the potential of their land by more clearing and enclosing, developing the cattle herds and by improved manuring. In 1560 we have a record of the Firle Estate of Sir John Gage supporting nearly 2,000 sheep and nearly 200 head of cattle.

Lewes' Michelmas sheep fair was the centre of the sheep marketing for East Sussex while, down along the river, the wharves were crammed with iron goods, woollen goods, wheat, and wood, all for trading out. For incoming trade, there were wines, silks, salt, fish and any amount of luxury goods for distributing, from overseas, around the county by sea and land and so on to London.

Squalor there may have been below stairs in Lewes. Above them, inflation was pushing values up everywhere and the world was becoming larger and more prosperous every day.

As a port, Lewes was also helped by the shifting of the Ouse outlet to the sea from Seaford, where it was becoming silted up, to the village of Meeching on the opposite side of the valley in 1539. Meeching then developed into the Newhaven of today, standing on the new channel cut from the river to the sea. At the same time the old, crumbling, wooden bridge over the Ouse, between Cliffe and the Eastgate of Lewes, was rebuilt. It was further repaired in the next century, 1650. It was rebuilt again in 1726 in brick and stone after floods had swept away the old structure of wood. It was widened in 1808 and in 1930/32.

The Cliffe Bridge crossing the River Ouse with the old warehouses down river.

However, a situation only eight miles up a navigable river did have one drawback. It was always vulnerable to attack from the sea. An attack by the French in 1377 had carried off the Prior of Lewes. A second attack in 1545 is commemorated in the wall-monument of Sir Nicholas Pelham who died in 1559, in St. Michael's Church:

"What time ye French sought to have sacked Seaford,
This Pelham did repell them back aboard,"

The pun would not have been lost on the Elizabethans . . . .

The Armada

Lewes was the centre for the organising of the placing and lighting of the warning beacons along the line of the Downs in the event of the threatened attacks from the sea. Firle Beacon and Ditchling Beacon still remember this in name. The beacons were not in the shape of bonfire stacks as visualised today. They consisted of a round tray full of burning material held up on a long pole supported at the bottom by tripod legs.

After the execution of Mary Queen of Scots, the threat from Spain loomed large and Lewes was the central point in Sussex, to prepare the defences against the anticipated Armada. Tensions ran high. No doubt the townsmen were called upon, by public proclamation, to bring out their armour and weapons for inspection. The "Twenty Four" were specifically ordered to do the same, as they did on each Whit Monday every year. The cannon and defences of the much depleted castle were put into readiness as well, and barrels of gunpowder were heaved up the steep mound and put into position.

As well for Lewes that the Spanish fleet was chivvied bravely from Plymouth, past the Isle of Wight and on up the Channel to Calais in that fateful week of July 20th-26th 1588 while the beacons flared from hilltop to hilltop along the watching coast. What the meagre defences of the little town would have made of the twenty-seven thousand men on board the one hundred and thirty galleons of Spain is a question happily not needing an answer.

The danger passed and the report and the smoke of cannon firing out at sea slowly drifted eastwards and Lewes breathed again. Then, as was her custom now, she celebrated the magnificent victory of England's gallant defenders in handsome style. The bonfires licked the night sky within rings of flaming torches, while the two large barrels of gunpowder were rammed endlessly into the castle cannon and shook the surrounding shops and houses to their very foundations with great explosions.

From the accession of Elizabeth, the annual lighting of bonfires had become a tradition in the town. It may indeed have not been wholly as a result of the martyrs' fires, but have been a relic of even earlier, traditional, apprentice celebrations. We have no records to confirm this either way. The Gunpowder Plot of 1605 merely reinforced the practice and gave it added point.

Local Government, Trade and Markets

Under the Tudors, local government and the local legal system became regularised further for the county and were entirely centred on Lewes. In the new Town Hall and Sessions House, built in stone in the High Street in 1546, the Justices of the Peace met four times a year on Quarter Days, as they had done, everywhere since the reign of Edward III (1388).

Their powers increased to cover the administration of wages and, later, of roads, bridges, corn supplies and even bastardy cases. After the dissolution of the monasteries, they became responsible for poor relief, an ever growing problem. The importance of the sheriff declined and the Lord Lieutenants, originally military figures, were appointed by the Crown to become honorary heads over the J.P.'s.

For purely town business and management, the Borough Court still met on the Monday following Michelmas for the election of Constables and to appoint the Clerks to administer the trade and industry of the town.

The new town hall took up a great deal of the roadway in the High Street. It was a long, regular, brick building roughly thirty feet long and twelve feet wide. It ran from the top of present day Station Street to the White Hart Hotel.

The ground floor was open to the street by rounded arches at both ends and a series of seven rounded arches at each side. For comparison, the old town halls of Rye and of Ludlow are of similar construction and still standing.

At the west end of the High Street, the West Gate still stood proud across the road with its constricted entrance only ten feet wide. From 1564, a Market House stood at the foot of the slope up to the Barbican through whose ground floor archways one entered the lane to the Barbican. The Titchfield market hall at the Weald and Downland Open Air Museum is of the same design.

What a congestion on market days! With sheep, cattle and horses all brought in to add to the conglomeration of stalls and jostling customers. Small wonder that a new market house was eventually designated in Market Street in 1792, where it still stands. The town hall stood until 1810 and, eighty years later, the Star Inn was converted and partly rebuilt to form the present day town hall.

The cattle market was held weekly in the High Street until 1879 and the Animal Fat Stock Show in Albion Street, off School Hill. By tradition also, oxen, bulls and cows were traded on St. Mark's Day, lean cattle on Whit Tuesday and sheep on St. Matthew's Day.

Lewes was the centre for the county trade and the farmers and their workers heaved or drove their goods along the rutted lanes of Sussex to sell or buy in the town. But there was also an outward movement. Carriers and pedlars took the goods from Lewes to the outlying villages, hamlets and farms. Their welcome arrival, by horse and cart or on foot, was a highlight in the week as far out as North Chailey, Ripe or Chiddingly. The carriers would take orders for cooking vessels, clothing and saddlery needs etc. and bring them out the following week. This trade flourished right into the 20th century. There are still people alive today who can remember the coming and going of the "Carrier from Lewes".

Non-conformity in Lewes

During the whole reign of Queen Elizabeth, underlying the growing prosperity of Lewes, was the continuing swing to Puritanism or Non-conformity which was to be such a feature of the town over the following centuries.

Under Edward VI (1548-1553), Lewes churches had been stripped bare of all their ornaments and statues. Even the stained glass in the windows had been wrenched out in the fervour of the New Religion. Elizabeth had endeavoured to keep a moderate balance betwen the growing number of Puritans and those who favoured the now established Church of England and the new Prayer Book. As long as they conformed outwardly, even Ministers of religion with known Puritan leanings were allowed to continue in office. The Crown was more concerned with the threat from the supporters of the old Catholicism which encompassed a very real feeling of treason.

Sir John Gage of Firle faced heavy fines and taxes for his Catholic leanings. The branch of the Gage family in residence at the outlying part of the estate, the Bentley Manor, now Bentley Wild Fowl, fared even worse as they were on the underground route for Catholic priests entering the country illegally and, being caught in the act, were reduced to real poverty. The other gentry in and around Lewes kept their heads in all senses of the term and conformed in public while their support for the Puritan persuasion increased.

They awaited the coming of the Scots King James with high hopes. He had acknowledged the Calvinist based Presbyterian Church in Scotland, surely he would be their leader in non-conformity in England. Perhaps the town's jubilation at the failure of the Gunpowder Plot was, in part due to this. There was an explosion of celebration far exceeding the bonfires that had marked the anniversary of the Queen's accession for the last forty-five years. Lewes marched to celebrate freedom. An indefinable freedom in many ways. Perhaps something too deep for words. Whatever it is, she celebrates it to this day, every November 5th. The finest Guy Fawkes night to be found anywhere in the world.

Guy Fawkes Night in Lewes

On November 5th in Lewes the shops shut early. The through traffic is firmly diverted. Apart from that, all are welcome. Thousands pour into the town from far and wide. All the surrounding towns hold their local celebrations on some other, prearranged, night throughout the Autumn for they too converge on Lewes with their Societies, their bands and their banners.

Lewes has six Bonfire Societies (originally eight) who have spent the whole year raising money and preparing for this night. It is they who organise the processions through the town from late afternoon until midnight. Up and down the dark streets they march, banners flying, bands re-echoing and a thousand torches flaring. The costumes of the marchers, many of rich and spectacular quality, are handed down from generation to generation as a treasured inheritance.

Symbolic barrels of tar on iron trolleys, burning hotly, are dragged down the length of School Hill to be thrown over the bridge parapet into the swirling Ouse. Wreaths are laid on the War Memorial and the town is alive with music and spectacle. Finally the Societies march to their appointed Bonfire sites followed by the streaming crowds in all directions and each stages a magnificent firework display for all to enjoy.

All are welcome, all is free. On Bonfire Night, every year, all Sussex comes to Lewes to share its celebrations, in cheerful and generous good humour, with whoever cares to join them. It is Sussex, and Lewes, at its greatest and best. Again, typically of the town, she quietly gives all the profits, next day, to the local Victoria Hospital and other charities, and clears up every single scrap of debris by 6 a.m. so that, walking through the town the next day, you might think it had only been a lovely dream . . . except that it happens all over again exactly one year later!

VIII.   LEWES IN THE SEVENTEENTH CENTURY

Alas for the non-conformists of Lewes, the King from Scotland had already had his fill of the domineering Calvinist-Presbyterians. Far from granting toleration of worship, one of his first acts, at the Hampton Court Conference in 1604-5, was to eject three hundred English Puritan clergy from their livings. For most of the next eighty-four years non-conformity was to be illegal and subject to penalties.

In search of religious freedom in 1620, the "Pilgrim Fathers" from Lincolnshire sailed from Plymouth. Others followed them from Norfolk down to Sussex. Lewes had plenty of contacts with the new Americas. One of the emigrants, a doctor from Ashford in Kent, settled in New England. He became, in time, a benefactor of Harvard University. His son, Comfort Star, eventually came back to live in England as a Congregational Minister in Lewes.

John Harvard, another American Puritan minister, who became posthumously, the founder of Harvard University, was married in the new church of South Malling, in 1636, to the daughter of the Rector of Ringmer, John Sadler. Lastly, later in the century, was Gulielma Marie Pothuma Springett, whose father, Sir William, was killed at the siege of Arundel in 1643. The Springetts, as already noted, were a leading family of Ringmer and Lewes. Gulielma became the wife of William Penn the Quaker, who founded Pennsylvania in 1681.

In 1681 William was given a grant of land beyond Delaware, in America, where the colony he founded, Pennsylvania, became famous for its toleration and freedom.

Lewes in America

There is, to this day, a Lewes, which is the County Town for Sussex, in Delaware U.S.A. It was first settled in 1659 by the Dutch and was known then by the unprepossessing name of "Whorekill". In 1674 it was ceded to the English and was part of Pennsylvania under William Penn. Being on the Delaware River, and near the coast, it was constantly harassed by the French in the Marlborough Wars of the early 18th century. Thus it had a good deal in common with its English counterpart.

It was not overly religious until much later, the first emigrants being more concerned with settling. But by 1728 the Scots and Irish had established Presbyterianism, the Quakers had a meeting-house and the Anglicans the Church of St. Peter. Life was harsh and the winters saw many of the stalwart settlers dying of the severe conditions of the 17th and 18th centuries in America. The settlement survived, however and, by 1909, it had become "Lewes, in the county of Sussex, in the State of Delaware", which it remains to this day.

The site of Lewes in America.

Back in England

During 1620-40 the suppression of the Puritans of Lewes continued unabated. But, as in the history of the Early Church, the more they suffered the stronger they grew.

"Conform", thundered the Crown and the Bishops . . . . But Lewes was far enough away from the centre of authority to keep her own council and think her own thoughts. One has only to look at the jury lists for the period to see how her mind, and those of her Sussex neighbours, worked, viz:- Weep-not-billing of Lewes, Called-lower of Warbleton, Thankful-Frewen of Northiam and Faint-not-Batchelor again of Lewes.

Records of the Archdeanery Court at Lewes show much slovenliness and decay in the fabric of the orthodox town churches. However there was no decay in the Puritan persuasion. They were, townsfolk, yeomen, burgesses, all "Calvinist to a man". In their pulpits they preached hours-long Puritan sermons to thirsting congregations. The gentry too, alarmed not only by the threat of religious oppression, but also by the political "divine right" claim of the first Stuart kings, and also their own loss of political prestige in Parliament, became more obviously supportive of the local Puritan cause. Lewes became known as a town "Tainted by Puritans".

The Civil War 1642-1649

To the Long Parliament (1642-1652) which heralded the opening of the Civil War, Sussex sent seventeen Roundhead representatives and eleven Cavaliers. Lewes returned two sturdy Puritans, Colonel Herbert Morley of Glynde and Colonel Anthony Stapely of Patcham. For the ten years of the hostilities between the two sides, Lewes was a firm stronghold for Parliament. Fortunately perhaps, Sussex mud and forest made widespread army manouevring well-nigh impossible. Lewes was to come through the war entirely unscathed.

However her defences were needfully arranged under Captain Ambrose Trayton and, in 1642, there was a threat to her safety when the Royalist Army came as near as Haywards Heath before being routed. Hastily two hundred volunteers were called to arms, and muskets and pikes were supplied. The racks for some of these are still in place in one of the fine houses at the bottom of School Hill.

Chichester and Arundel, in West Sussex, were both besieged and captured in 1664. It was in the latter siege that Sir William Springett of Ringmer received his fatal wounds in the cross-fire. When the loyal Parliamentarian lay dying, his wife (expectant mother of the Gulielma already mentioned) hastened down from London to his death-bed. The roads were flooded, the coach broke down, and she was thrown out in the dark into a hedge. Finally she finished the journey, doggedly, on foot and reached her dying husband just before his end. Later, happily to relate, she found a second husband, a Mr Isaac Pennington, the friend of William Penn who was to marry her daughter.

The Springetts, as a Ringmer family, were very familiar with the difficulties of travel in Sussex. Sir William's father, Herbert Springett who died in 1620, is traditionally remembered as the gentleman who, finding the road to church one Sunday too muddy for his horses, determinedly yoked eight oxen to his carriage and arrived, triumphantly on time.

But Lewes, like all Sussex, was not eager to be involved in hostilities on either side. The conflict was essentially one between the lesser gentry and clergy, who supported Parliament, and the Crown who were supported, in the main, by the higher gentry. The peasants certainly had little to gain, whoever won. They were liable to be unwillingly impressed to fight on either side. Their crops and animals were seized without redress when needed. All this, together with bad harvests, low wages and the Government's five-percent tax on food, led to riots in the Weald, always a wild, rough and lawless place at the best of times. A Parliamentary recruiting officer was beaten up at West Hoathly Fair in 1643.

Said an exasperated army leader, "Sussex is full of neuters and malignants".

When the fighting was over at last, ten gentry from Sussex were among the judges on the King, led by Herbert Morley and Anthony Stapely. However none of them signed his death warrant in 1649.

But for Lewes, the Civil War, and in fact the whole Stuart Period, was essentially one of religious interest. She had swung so far over to the Puritan way of thinking that freedom of worship seemed a much more worthwhile cause for contest than constitutional or political matters.

More Non-conformity in Lewes

The first two Stuart kings had tried hard to impose the Church of England as a rigid orthodoxy on the Country. In 1639, just before war broke out, there were official reports of "Some little trouble about Lewes" adding that "Sussex was not so much troubled with Puritan Ministers (many of whom had been suppressed anyway) as with Puritan Justices of the Peace".

When the Puritans came into their own, half way through the war, the situation was completely reversed. Parliament, which was in control, from 1643 to 1649, ordered an Assembly at Westminster of "Godly and learned divines" to re-establish the Presbyterian system as the Church of the Land. Lewes sent her leading Puritan minister, the Reverend Benjamin Pickering of St. Mary's, Westout, to have a share in the administration.

Now the Presbyterians became as bigoted in their way as the Anglicans, and earlier the Roman Catholics, had been in theirs. All the Anglican ministers were ejected from *their* churches. Worse still, for the man in the street, all liberty of speech was forbidden and life became restricted, narrow, bleak and colourless.

It was inevitable that some reaction should ensue. It came in the form of a rising new religious party calling themselves The Independents who, under the increasing prestige of Oliver Cromwell, came to dominate Parliament and the Roundhead army. In Lewes in 1647, an Independent became Rector at the central church of St. Michael's, the Reverend Gwalter Postlethwaite, while, throughout all England under Cromwell, between 1649 and 1659, tolerance replaced bigotry at last. There was toleration of a sort for all, except for the Roman Catholic followers and sects that advocated priests as opposed to pastors.

Puritans everywhere now disjointed themselves into an astonishing number of different sects. These called themselves Baptists, Seekers and Quakers etc. The Seekers had a small group at Southover, but most of them eventually joined with the newly-formed Quakers.

The Quakers were founded by George Fox in 1655. In Lewes the movement originated at the house of John Russell in Southover. It spread rapidly across the county. George Fox, with his friend Alexander Parker, had journeyed to Lewes from Steyning where John Launder had been burned as a martyr in 1555. They then journeyed on to Warbleton, the tiny village from which had come the most famous of the Lewes martyrs, Richard Woodman.

At first the Quakers were riotously violent in their outbursts of protest in public places and at church services. They incurred much early enmity in Lewes and often found themselves clapped in Horsham Gaol. On one occasion, when they were holding a meeting on "The Castle Green", now Castle bowling-green, they were set on by the local Independents with "swords, guns and pikes" to their great discomfort.

This hot-headed side of the Quakers quickly cooled however. They then became the determinedly peace-loving peoples that we know still today. They remained firmly entrenched in Lewes and we remember that George Fox's most famous follower, William Penn, found his wife, as has already been told, in Ringmer.

In 1675 the Quakers were meeting in Thomas Moseley's house in the Cliffe. The Cliffe or Southover were invariably the districts that cradled the new sects. In 1784 they built, and moved into, what is now the very lovely, timber furnished, Friends Meeting House along Friars Walk. It is a low, tiled building, decorated with mathematical tiles and two-coloured brickwork. The surrounding garden is a haven of peace and colour and, among the grass and the flowerbeds, contains thirty-eight headstones of local worthies.

Oliver Cromwell died in 1659. The following year, it was at Lewes that the curtain was finally rung down on the Civil War and the Commonwealth. For it was in a Lewes merchant's ship, and from the Lewes quayside, that his son and heir, Richard Cromwell, escaped to the Continent in the autumn of 1660, probably through the good offices of Colonel Morley of Glynde.

The Stuart royal family was restored to the throne, but the hopes of the Non-conformists for a more tolerant religious policy from Charles II were savagely dashed by the passing of the Act of Uniformity in 1662. By this the Anglicans now took their revenge on the Presbyterians who had turned them out of office in the last decade. Two thousand non-conforming leaders were summarily evicted from their livings.

At St. Mary's, Westout, the Reverend Edward Newton, who had succeeded Mr Pickering, took a most sorrowful leave of his flock. At St. Michael's Church, Mr Postlethwaite similarly bade farewell to his congregation. They were later forbidden to even reside within five miles of their churches, and five miles would have seemed a great deal further in 1665 than it does to us today. It rendered continuing communication with their followers all but impossible.

But the sturdy Non-conformists of Lewes were by no means cowed or beaten. In 1669 at least five hundred Presbyterians met at South Malling in secret. The Independents still gathered to worship at another secret rendezvous in the Parish of All Saints. While a third sect, "about sixty" it is reported, gathered somewhere in the Cliffe. Their courage bore fruit and, in 1672, the law relaxed sufficiently to allow public worship for them providing they applied for a licence which, in Lewes, they did, sending Mr Newton to London to obtain it. Finally, under William and Mary, the Toleration Act of 1689 gave freedom of worship to all Dissenters except the Roman Catholics and the Unitarians.

Obviously its religious struggles had in no way dampened the spirit and cheerfulness of the Lewes townsfolk. For, after the national scare of the Titus Oates Plot of 1679, in Charles II's reign, the town held a tremendous bonfire celebration on the November 5th of that year. It was, understandably, still predominantly anti-Catholic, the threat of a return to Catholicism, under the Stuarts, being particularly strong.

The streets were loudly paraded by young men armed with swords and muskets marching under anti-Jesuit banners. The Pope accompanied by Guy Fawkes in effigy, was followed by caricatures of clergy and friars, one pretending to sprinkle holy water on to the crowds with a bottle brush. Finally all was committed to the flames in a huge town bonfire.

Twenty years later, in 1699, the first official Presbyterian meeting house was established in the town. Mr Newton was joined by the Reverend Thomas Barnard from Glyndebourne to officiate to the Presbyterian congregation. Mr Barnard, a man of vision and energy, bought the Bull House, originally the Goring mansion, by the West Gate, and transformed the south of it into the Westgate Chapel. It opened on November 5th, surely a most auspicious date, in 1700. It was to this chapel that the Reverend Comfort Star, or Starr, later gravitated from the new lands across the Atlantic.

The remainder of the building was sold off as a separate residence, now the Bull House and beautifully restored in 1922 by a public-minded Alderman, John Every, owner of the Phoenix Ironworks in the Cliffe, who then gave it to the Sussex Archaeological Society for preservation. On a fire-back in a splendid original, open fireplace in the house is inscribed a potted version of its eventful history:-

> "Here stands the Bull within the West Gate,
> Sir Henry Goring changed its state.
> He built a house when Bess was Queen.
> Which Westgate Chapel since has been.
> The Bull for Thomas Paine found room.
> John Every saved it from its doom."
>   1922

"Gentlemen's seats ... with their gardens". This view of Lewes Castle still giving something of the same impression in the 20th century.

IX. EARLY GEORGIAN LEWES

One can imagine that Lewes heaved a sigh of relief as the wheels of time turned and the old century faded into the new. Civil war was already a generation behind, Protestantism in all its varied forms was an accepted way of worship, and an exciting New World was beginning to stretch out to limitless horizons across the seas.

Behind her, over the Wealden forest, coal from much further away in England and Wales replaced wood as fuels. Other iron deposits too now supplied the furnaces in Shropshire and the North-east and, later, the Welsh valleys. Charcoal-burning persisted until almost modern times but the heavy clanging of iron and the rumbling of the huge carts bearing cannon and shot not longer grooved the Wealden "clegg" to Lewes.

Life in the already over-big spread of London, fifty miles to the north, was over-crowded, dirty and smelly in spite of the fine new building in the City centre by Inigo Jones and Sir Christopher Wren. The narrow, cobbled streets were full, by day, with carts and coaches, street-sellers shouting, and horses and dogs everywhere.

At night they were dark and dangerous places. Thieves and footpads lurked in the unlit alleys and Hogarth's picture of gin-swilling men and women outside the run-down ale-house is not that far off the mark.

But Lewes, despite the fact that she could boast of fifty inns and ale-houses (in Victorian times it was over seventy!), was a quiet and rather elegant little town by all accounts. Prosperous too. Daniel Defoe the author, describes it on his travels as "Full of the seats of gentlemen of good families and fortune".

In 1730, it was again said to be "Chiefly composed of gentlemen's seats, joining one to another, with their gardens adjoining". Looking up at Lewes from the southern aspect, it still gives the same impression, as garden-trees and garden-walls seem to mount the slope from the Grange Gardens to the foot of the Castle.

There are a number of interesting factors to account for this appearance of "comfortable 18th century dignity". Firstly Lewes was set in the centre of a varied and prosperous countryside. "The richest and most profitable in all that part of England", says Defoe. Until not so long ago the stock was still driven in to market on the hoof and the streets were awash with mud and "muck". Those iron foot-scrapers assigned to every cottage front tell their own tale.

Secondly, when the Church of the Land was slipping into sad decline, Lewes folk were predominantely and enthusiastically non-conformist (dissenters as they were often called). Puritan in outlook and behaviour, they were intensely earnest both in their principles of faith and of living. A Mr William Ridge writes of an ordination service held at the Westgate Chapel on July 21st, 1742: "Whole Service was about four hours and a half . . . !" Also, being banned from academic life or any sort of public service, they had no choice but to make their living by trade, industry and property at which they proved extremely successful.

Profits were ploughed back into purchasing more town and country property and improving it. The Springetts of Ringmer owned several houses and shops on School Hill and along the High Street. Later, in 1782, Thomas Kemp (son of the owner of Barbican House) became an evangelical preacher and a property tycoon. There were Quaker ship-builders, wool-merchants, timber-merchants, iron-mongers . . . They worked hard, they prospered, and the town prospered with them.

We climb to the topmost end of the social scale to find the third reason for that most pleasing appearance of early 18th century Lewes. The gentry. In rural England, which encompassed 80% of the population at this time, the power of the King had been successfully reduced by the 17th century Civil War and the succeeding Glorious Revolution. The vacuum resulting had been neatly filled by a new land-owning aristocracy who were to dominate the government of the Country for the next century and a half.

In many cases they were the same gentry whom we have seen gaining wealth, particularly through the Tudor Age, by clever finance, resourceful marriage

Fine Georgian facades on School Hill.

and also by forcible enclosures of neighbouring common-land. With money and leisure they embarked on the "Grand Tour" of Europe and came home with their heads filled with visions of Versailles, of Florence and of Rome. Their returning luggage bulged with treasures in marble, bronze and gold.

They began to build, or to rebuild, their country seats in the new styles, the Venetian Palladian or the Roman Classic. They demanded the large and well-proportioned windows of the French palaces, the stately porticos of Italy and the stone parapets and cornices that gave such a handsome finish to the uncluttered facings. Firle Park, Ashburnham, Glynde Place, Halland House (now no more), Stanmer Park (1724), and the smaller mansions such as Coombe Place, Offham (1730) and Shelley's Folly (1702) — Sussex is a treasure-house of their building still.

It was a status-symbol of course, but a fine one. As also was the vast surrounding parkland and the imposing, mile-long drive up to the classic portico. The age of the great landscape gardeners, Thomas Repton and Capability Brown was at hand.

The "new-look" naturally penetrated the towns. In Lewes, Pelham House was refashioned externally in the latest style in 1720. Newcastle House was built opposite the redesigned Town Hall in the important centre of the High Street in 1717. Further up the street, Barbican House, just below the Castle, was refaced and given a fine doric doorway before it came to Thomas Kemp of Kemp Town, Brighton, fame.

Beyond the West Gate, Shelleys was remodelled in equally fine style and, on the opposite side of the road, St. Anne's House was raised elegantly in brick in 1719. All the houses on this side of the street date from the later 18th century and descend from St. Anne's church to the typically rounded Georgian corner-piece opposite Antioch House in charming, modest, Georgian succession. From here to the White Hart again, many of the frontages are of the latter half of the 18th century and with a wealth of mathematical tiling for which Lewes is justly famous.

At the same time too, the Star Inn was magnificently refurbished in the latest fashion, inside and out, by its proprietor. Within, he replaced the staircase with the present exceedingly fine Jacobean staircase from the derelict Slaugham Manor. The outside received a very splendid Georgian facing. The Star, being the most important hostelry, covered a surprisingly large area, not only for the accommodation of travllers, but also for their carriages and horses as well. A popular inn of this period might well provide stabling for up to six hundred animals.

Down School Hill the fine Georgian facades are intermittently continued, some in brick like School Hill House (refaced in 1715) which has another splendid staircase locally crafted. Some are faced with mathematical tiles as are those standing opposite. Lewes House was unfortunately refaced in the 19th century, but a turn down Church Twitten to glimpse the garden front will reveal the 18th century design and workmanship.

Still descending, across the road, where solicitors offices now abound, is a complete series of dignified Georgian frontages continued into the lower part of the High Street in Dial House (c. 1740) rebuilt by one of the Quaker family of Rickman who were bankers, brewers, ship-builders and merchants, and many of whom lie buried in the Meeting-House garden in Friars Walk.

The old Medieval West Gate, at the top of the High Street, was at last pulled down in 1763. By this date only the ruined towers had been left standing and are said to have been pulled down for a wager.

Eighteenth century Lewes was nothing if not thorough in her modernisation. The old Market Hall was demolished and rebuilt in 1793 on the site of three houses adjoining the Crown Inn. The old Town Bell, inscribed as "Gabriel", which had been removed in 1761 from the remaining church tower of the long demolished St. Nicholas Church, which had stood near the present War Memorial, was now re-hung in the tower adjoining the new Market.

This would certainly have given a much clearer aspect to the centre of this now predominately Georgian town. Perhaps the most interesting memorial of all lies in the little regarded, and still less understood, carved stone plaque on the former Eastgate Stoneworks (1823) almost opposite the Eastgate Baptist Chapel. This reads "Established over a Century", and in fact commemorates the Morris family who were masons of 18th and 19th century Lewes.

Arthur Morris was mason at Stanmer Park from 1722 to 1726. He also built the new stone bridge at Lewes over the Ouse in 1727. He was Constable for the town in 1725, 1736, and 1741. His son, John, who was also Constable in 1751 and 1765, was the mason for Glynde Church and Glynde Place in 1750, Ashburnham Place from 1757 to 1761, the Sessions House in Lewes in 1761, and for Pelham House in Lewes and Firle Place.

With their apprentices, Parsons and Bridgman, their memorials embellish churches and churchyards throughout Sussex. We have much to remember them for.

A last interesting feature of 18th century Lewes was a garden that was laid out high up on Cliffe Hill in the true spirit of the period. While Londoners paraded in their fashionable Vauxhall Gardens, Lewes folk breathlessly climbed what we now call Cuilfail to enjoy the delights of Baldy's Garden. This was established by Thomas Baldy (1710-82), a china merchant. The view from here is still superb of town, valley and downland although the garden is no more.

While Lewes was updating her building in the latest Georgian style, other changes were also taking place. The old rule of "The Twelve" had been suppressed by Charles II and never regained its former status. The town Constables were now chosen by the Steward of the current Lord of Lewes and the Court leet. The Justices of the Peace were still appointed by the Crown. In effect they were all chosen and manipulated by the wealthiest and most energetic, local landowner at the time. For Lewes, this was the head of the Pelham family.

By 1700 the Pelhams had become exceedingly prosperous. Thomas had become Lord Pelham in 1706. His eldest son became the Duke of Newcastle in 1715. In the two-party system of the day, the latter was a Whig, becoming eventually the leader of the party in which he held state offices for over forty-six years. During this time he not only ruled East Sussex, from Lewes, but, for a number of years ruled all England as well, being twice Prime Minister.

He lived mainly in his Queen Anne style mansion at nearby Halland which had superseded Laughton Place. He also possessed a mansion at Bishopstone. His passage from the one to the other across the Sussex countryside was heralded by the ringing of church bells en route . . . and the clanging of deferential scythes and ploughshares at Glynde where there were no church bells! It was royal state.

His brother, Henry, built his baronial seat at Stanmer near Brighton, now Stanmer Park. Sir Henry's son succeeded to the title of Newcastle on the death of his uncle and became the Earl of Chichester in 1801 for "services to the sovereign", George III.

Sussex elected twenty-four members of Parliament, two for the county as a whole and twenty-two from the separate boroughs. In fact, one of the County members was always a Pelham nominee and the other was chosen by agreement with the other large landowners of the County. The two representatives for Lewes were similarly controlled by the Duke of Newcastle.

To our liberated ears this may sound highly immoral, but in 18th century rural England it suited the times well. The landowners, who numbered seventy for the whole of England, were essentially rural-minded. They all possessed London town houses, but their interests lay in the countryside and their rule was a benevolent despotism. They gave enormous employment locally and wealthy patronage. There was a safety about the whole system that agreed well with this first half century when England was settling herself into a new position of internal peace and growing World, and worldly, importance.

Below the local magnate came the local squire and the local parson, the latter now often a younger son of the aristocracy. The squire owned substantial holdings and had much in common with the larger landowners. Further down the scale, the yeoman was the properous middle-class farmer. Lastly, there was the peasantry with abysmally low living standards. In Sussex however the peasants did have other financially-rewarding interests, namely smuggling.

The Smugglers

Smuggling, in the 18th century, along the whole south-east coast of England, was possibly the largest source of employment of the day, or rather should one say, the night.

Lewes, with her wealth of old Medieval crypts and her cellars and tunnels through the soft chalk, not to mention the River Ouse lapping her feet, was admirably equipped for the smuggling industry. It had been an accepted way of life ever since taxes and tolls were first imposed by the iron-fisted Normans.

Through the Middle Ages, the "Owlers" dealt mainly in wool. In Tudor times and under the Stuarts, the cargo was wool, together with armaments, recusants and dissenters. in the 18th century, the rise of wealth and the demand for luxury goods founded the Golden Age of smuggling in Sussex. Now it was for silk and tea, snuff, wines and spirits etc., all far easier to transport than wool or cannon or even people. The returns were that much more profitable and the loads much more readily concealed.

Everybody was concerned, from the great landowners down to the unemployed iron-worker. There was "Brandy for the parson and baccy for the clerk", silks and tea for the burgesses, snuff and laces for the aristocracy. It was a profession for hundreds and a highly lucrative one. It required good organisation to transport the bulk of the goods firstly across the water and then over fifty miles of countryside from the Coast to London which was the Mecca of the trade. But the pay, at an average of half a guinea for a day and a night's work, was more than tempting when a labourer might only earn twenty pounds, lawfully, in a whole year and, if unemployed, could expect only a parish hand-out or starvation.

The smuggling gangs of Sussex are famous, particularly the Hawkhurst Gang and that from Alfriston. Very little was ever heard of Lewes' smuggling activities. She, as usual, kept her own council and discretion. But we have on record that, in 1731, the dragoons were dispatched to Lewes against the smugglers and, at another time, a "smuggler riding furiously through Lewes when drunk, killed his horse by mounting the pavement".

In 1780, Lewes folk were brought from their beds in alarm when loud firing was heard coming from the Channel. But when it was discovered to be an engagement between the King's cutter, manned by the excise men, and two smuggling cutters . . . and the latter were winning . . . Lewes returned to bed well satisfied.

An old pamphlet of the East Grinstead Assizes of 1748 details the trade well:- "Each man is allowed half a guinea a time. Also his expenses for eating and drinking, and a horse is found for him. He shall also get the profits of a Dollop of Tea (13 pounds in weight) which is half a bag. The total profit should therefore be 24 or 25 shillings. They always make one, sometimes two journeys a week."

But the Law was savage to those who were caught. They were condemned to death and hung in chains as a grisly warning to others, although this did nothing to put a stop to such a lucrative employment. Only the lessening of taxes on the goods involved and the introduction of Income Tax as a safer and much easier substitute for the gathering of revenue did that. At the same time, after the Napoleonic Wars which ended in 1815, the Navy was free to assist the coast-guards and excise-men in patrolling the coasts. And so the great age of Sussex and Lewes smuggling passed into history.

Pastimes of Lewes

By day, Georgian Lewes was still its peaceable, Law-abiding self. It was, above all things, a great centre for talk. The first local newspaper, the Lewes Journal, went into publication in 1745. The present Newcastle House, built by Benjamin Court, an iron-monger from the Cliffe, became the most popular of the Coffee-houses of the town when, in 1717, it was taken over by the Duke of Newcastle and transformed into a centre for the Whig Club in Lewes, a splendid place for all his supporters to gather, to argue and to plan.

Across the road, in the White Hart was another leading rendezvous for the town. This became known as the "Headstrong Club". Here the members had a custom of handing the most vociferous and successful arguer of the evening the "Headstrong Book". Thomas Paine, the revolutionary, was often to be handed it during his six years stay in Lewes.

Not all was talk and argument however. It was through the influence of the Duke of Newcastle that the Assizes were established in Lewes. The new Assize Courts, or Crown Courts, were built later, in the early 1800's, next door to Newcastle House in imposing Classical style faced with Portland stone.

A house of correction was built in North Street in 1793, complete with a treadmill which worked a mill. It housed an average of one hundred offenders at a time. This was said to have replaced a smaller house in the Cliffe (No. 59) which was in use from 1612 to 1796. That in North Street subsequently gave way to the County Gaol. It was later a Naval prison, as the plaque on it records, and was demolished in 1963.

The Duke bought up a considerable amount of property in the town, including the Pelham Arms and, through incredibly lavish expenditure, bought votes at every election.

Even more profitable to the town was the rivalry between the Duke, as a Whig, and the Tory leader, Thomas Sergison. They spent to out-manoeuvre each other and the town happily enjoyed the proceeds. It was Sergison who remodelled the Star Inn so extravagantly to give his Tory supporters a centre to rival the Whig Rooms in Newcastle House. Disraeli and William Cobbett, in time, both visited and debated here.

Second to politics, in the passions of the wealthy, came a love of horses and horse racing. It is an obvious fact that the horse loomed as large in the life of the 18th century man as the car achieves importance in the life of 20th century man. Deer-hunting had given way to fox-hunting. The last deer-park in the area had been the Broyle Park at Ringmer which was one of the few enclosures, locally, of the 18th century, another being the Dicker Common north of Ripe and Chalvington.

Fox-hunting in Sussex was not just an exciting sport involving horses, it was a social occasion for the gentry. With the full stretch of the South Downs at their disposal, it was a favourite occupation of all riding folk. It is still popular today, the Southdown Hunt kennels being based at Ringmer, three miles outside Lewes.

Whatever one's personal feelings are on blood-sports, (and it is a well-known fact that the Sussex fox is immeasurably cleverer than the Sussex horse, hound or huntsman), it is well worth a visit to Lewes on Boxing Day to witness a time-honoured spectacle. For then the Southdown Hunt congregates, in all its colourful glory, at the White Hart Hotel and rides, immaculately, up the full length of the town to the Victoria Hospital at the foot of Racecourse Hill. Here it re-musters before a leisurely trot over the Downs until mid-afternoon. The sight of the entire Hunt riding abreast the road, led by the hound-packs, and the sound of the hooves and the jingling of harness is a picturesque tradition of Lewes history that is still very much part of the town.

Before we leave these halcyon days of the first half of the 18th century, mention should be made of the doctors, for many of them played a distinguished part in daily life through the centuries. Disease was prevalent everywhere in Lewes, as it was, and always had been, in society. Polluted well-water, fleas, and lice, joined with the total lack of safe sanitation to breed a continuing supply of fever, plague and running sores.

Barber-surgeons are represented, under the Tudors, by Thomas Blunt (died 1611) one of the "Twelve" and the presenter of the fine silver-gilt cup to the town, still to be seen among the treasures in the Town Hall. Among the named Dissenters of the 17th century are the barber-surgeons William Humphrey and John Snashall. A Doctor Tabor lived in Lewes House at the end of the century and, in St. Michael's parish lived the brilliant Doctor Russell. It was Dr. Russell who first advocated, in his pamphlet of 1750, drinking and bathing in sea-water to prevent, or cure, tuberculosis, tooth-decay and intestinal disorders. He then moved from Lewes to Brighton to establish a hydro on the site of the present Albion Hotel and thus unaugurated the phenomenal growth of that town from that date onwards.
He married William Kemp's daughter and heiress, of Malling Deanery, where he lived also until his move to Brighthelmstone. he died in 1759 in London and is buried in Malling. There is a plaque to his memory on the wall of No. 78 in Lewes High Street.

Dr. Frewen, son of 'Thankful Frewen" the Rector of Northiam, also practised in Lewes until 1769. He published a book on inoculation against small-pox in 1749. In 1794 2,890 persons were inoculated in Lewes four years before Jenner's discovery of a small-pox vaccine in 1798. Forty-six of these died as a result but perhaps they would have succumbed, regardless, as until 1800 8% of every generation was estimated to die of the "pox".

Lastly we remember Gideon Mantell who, like Dr. Russell was a Fellow of the Royal Society. He was apprenticed to Dr. James Moore who practised at Castle Place. Mantell eventually formed the two centre houses of Castle Place for his own residence and added the ammonite motif on the doorway which is still such a feature. He was a great physician and is even more famous as a geologist, hence the ammonites.

In doctoring, Lewes was an epitome of the times. There was a great improvement in professional skills throughout the Country as a whole in the 18th century. This was the age when nearly all the great London hospitals were founded. Guys, Westminster, St. George's, the London Hospital and the Middlesex Hospital were all established between 1720 and 1745. In Lewes, a Borough Pest House was established in 1742 on the site of the old St. Nicholas' Hospital at St. Anne's for the current scourge of small-pox.

With a notable number of members of the Royal Society among her townsfolk, particularly her physicians, perhaps it is not so suprising that, in 1926, Lewes should suddenly realise that it stood on the nought-degree Line of Longitude, the Meridian graduation on the globe that had first been instituted by that same Royal Society.

Lewes was the first town to be aware of, and commemorate, the fact. An interesting pillar surmounted by an astrolabe, stands in Meridian Road at the entrance to the Landport Estate, which marks the crossing. There is also a line set into the pavement in Western Road near the Black Horse Inn to mark the passage of the line through the town.

X.   LEWES IN THE AGE OF REASON

The Age of Contentment, as the first half of the 18th century may well be called, lasted almost exactly for the fifty years assigned to it. Then the barometer of life in the Western World changed alarmingly. The pointer swung to "change" and ominously forecast "storms, upheavals and revolution". In 1756 the Seven Years War broke out between England and France. Before it ended, in 1763, it had engulfed Europe, North America, the West Indies and West Africa.

Following this there were, in quick succession, no less than four revolutions. On the home-front there was revolutionary change in Agriculture and later in Industry. Overseas, the American War of Independence (1775-1777) was followed by the French Revolution in 1789, all upheavals that shook the civilised World.

Thomas Paine

Lewes no doubt discussed the news avidly as it came in on the stage-coach to the Star, and the White Hart. Little was it realised that, from 1768 until 1774, the seed of two of these revolutions was actually living in the town. Thomas Paine was the man in question, born the son of a Quaker in Thetford in 1737.

Paine was one of the first of a long line of "radicals". From the age of thirteen he was a rolling stone who eventually came to rest with the Quaker owner of Bull House, Westgate, Lewes in 1768. By this time he had become an Excise-man for the second time. The first time he had been dismissed for "discrepancies in the books".

Being an Excise-man was as poorly paid and as unpopular with the law-breakers then as the tax-inspector is today. Paine spent all his moments off-duty down at the White Hart Inn arguing unendingly with the other hot-heads of the town.

The "Headstrong Book" was won by him so often that it received an added official title: "The Headstrong Book or Original Book of Obstinacy, Written by . . . of Lewes in Sussex and Revised and corrected by Thomas Paine". He preached "Rights for all and Down with the Rich". Lewes heard him with interest but she was too inured to the interminable harangues of her non-conformist preachers to be over impressed. Besides he was an Excise-man and the local industry was smuggling!

He married his host's daughter Elizabeth. Then his enthusiasm for the under-dog cost him his job. He supported a claim for higher pay by his fellow excise-men and was firmly removed from their ranks for good by the Establishment. In 1774 he left Lewes, and his wife, and eventually travelled to the American colonies where his book, "Commonsense", stirred many of the wavering colonists to outright revolution and did much to add a final spark to the outbreak of the War for American Independence.

In 1787 he removed to France where he threw himself wholeheartedly into yet another revolution and published "The Rights of Man" in 1791. However he ended up in a Paris prison awaiting the guillotine. His oratory had made him few friends. He only narrowly escaped the hideous knife at the plea of the American Ambassador. He found refuge back across the Atlantic again where he died, a pauper, in New York in 1809.

Before he died he described the 18th century as "The Age of Reason". It was a perceptive title although much of Paine's own reasoning was unwise for he had the narrow, enthusiastic bigotry of many revolutionaries. Some of his writings however have an intriguingly prophetic ring of wisdom for, among his visionary proposals were, incredibly:- Graduated income-tax, education for all, old-age pensions and maternity benefits!

In his lonely old age in America he remembered again his stay in Lewes. He wrote to his old friends of the White Hart days, "Since my departure from Lewes, fortune and providence have thrown me into a line of action which my first setting out in life could not have possible suggested. . . I still pursue, and ever will, the same path. . . the path of Liberty."

Lewes carefully remembers him with a kindly plaque on the wall of the Bull House and also at the White Hart Hotel.

The French Revolution

During the French Revolution (1789-93), Lewes again played host to the many emigres shipping by packet to Newhaven in fear for their lives. Many too, were given shelter in the great houses of Sussex.

At Sheffield Park, the Compte de Lally was the guest of the First Lord Sheffield and his daughter Maria Josepha for a considerable time. Maria writes in her diary of an occasion when a group of priests also arrived, sole survivors of a massacre in a French convent. They sat around the fire in the book-lined library at Sheffield Park House, still shivering from their ordeal and telling and retelling the Earl and the Compte of their terrifying escape.

Lord Sheffield was a newcomer to Sussex having moved down from Yorkshire in 1769 when he purchased Sheffield Park and had a new mansion built on the Tudor foundations in the latest "Gothick" style by James Wyatt. The gardens were laid out by Capability Brown and Humphrey Repton. At the turn of the half-century both the Pelham brothers had died, Thomas in 1768 and Henry in 1754. Their places in Lewes and in Sussex politics were then largely taken over by Lord Sheffield and the Duke of Richmond (from Goodwood). Both brought genuine concern and good administration abilities into local affairs especially in trade, industry and matters concerning defence.

Lewes, like England as a whole, in spite of nurturing Thomas Paine was too old and wise to be drawn into another political revolution. But the contribution of a near neighbour at Glynde to the Agricultural Revolution of the late 1700's was considerable, and also very profitable to Lewes itself.

Developments in Agriculture

The Agricultural Revolution during the 18th and 19th centuries bought about improvements in knowledge of animal breeding, soil enrichment, and in cropping.

In total it doubled the agricultural output of the country which was providential as the poulation, due mainly to improved medicine, had also doubled during the same time. By 1801 the Lewes population had risen to 5,257.

In Sussex, Glynde is a very pretty little Downland village which nestles under the eastern skirts of Mount Caburn. John Ellman (1753-1832) came here in 1761 from Hartfield. He established himself as a yeoman farmer running sheep and cattle on the chalk slopes and along Glynde Reach. Following the example of Bakewell in Leicestershire, he bred his sheep selectively until he had built up a "Southdown" flock that gave more meat and more wool per animal than any contemporary animal. His successful methods attracted great interest, spreading over much of the South-east and led to increased farm production particularly in wool. The increased trade that followed converged naturally on the fairs, markets and quays of Lewes.

Ellman was a man of forward ideas in may aspects of farming and also in welfare. Autocratic in his village, he forbade the presence of an ale-house in the district. But to his farm workers he was a considerate and generous employer. The unmarried workers he boarded in his own farmhouse. Those who married he set up in their own cottage complete with a garden plot for their vegetables, chickens and pig. He was an enthusiastic local cricketer and also maintained a village school for the children of his employees. His grave and memorial stone can be seen in the churchyard of the Classic Glynde church.

A government survey for the end of the century (1801) gives some idea of the enormous importance of the animal husbandry in the County. It shows a total of 350,000 sheep, twice the human population, also 63,000 pigs, 60,000 head of cattle and 22,000 horses. Many of which, at some time or another, went through the markets of Lewes.

The regular livestock markets for cattle, sheep and horses still took place in the High Street. There was also a large County Annual Fat-stock Show in Albion Street established by Lord Egremont of Petworth.

A huge Sheep Fair was also now held on the Downs, on the old Battle-ground of 1264, every Michelmas. This attracted up to 50,000 sheep at a time. It is no longer held, but a visit to Findon, in West Sussex, in the Autumn, will demonstrate its modern equivalent. In addition a large Wool Fair was established under the patronage of Lord Sheffield on the 20th of July. Southdown fleeces were "very highly esteemed".

The corn trade moved from the Market House, below the Castle, to the Star Inn in 1792 when the Market House was pulled down, while in the new market at the top of North Street, now Market Street, provisions were traded weekly.

Trading of all this produce brought much wealth to Lewes, much of the profits being invested in town properties, banking houses and local transport improvements, for this was also the age of the Turnpike roads and the building of canals. In the late 18th century, Lewes rode richly on the back of the Southdown sheep.

She even had her famous shepherds. One in particular was John Dudney, born in Plumpton in 1782. For years, from a small boy, he had tended his master's sheep, living in his mobile shepherd's hut on the lonely downs over Newmarket Hill. He had plenty of time for meditation and thought in his solitary existence, which he put to the excellent use of teaching himself mathematics and languages. The latter included Hebrew. In the soft chalk of the hill side he dug out a "study" for himself and there he kept his small library of books.

His enthusiasm for learning proved so successful that he eventually came to leave his shepherding life altogether and set up as a schoolmaster in the town of Lewes. He lived along Abinger Place, in Milton House, and here he opened the school that he ran for many years until he died at the age of seventy.

The Turnpike Roads

As already mentioned above, developments in other spheres necessarily led to the need for improvements in transport. The first Sussex Turnpike Trust for improving roads in the County was set up in 1749.

The turnpike roads were mainly investments by the local men of substance who looked for their returns to be obtained from the tolls levied at the toll-gates:- "For every wagon drawn by six horses or oxen: 1/6d. For calves, sheep etc.: 5d. and so on. The oxen, interestingly were of black, Welsh stock, not the characteristic brown Sussex ox of today. They were driven down to the local markets all the way, on the hoof, by Welsh drovers and were shod for roadwork just as the horse is today.

The hill into Lewes over the edge of Malling Down had always presented a difficult and dangerous road and was the scene of many accidents to coaches and farm wagons. In the last days of these road improvements, the high track that had climbed up the side of the Down and then down again into the town was lowered fifteen feet. The hazardous stretch of centuries thus became the Malling Hill of today and, in the making, turned up some gruesome relics of the ancient history of the town in the form of twenty human skeletons. These were complete with iron spearheads, sword blades and iron shield bosses. They were identified as the valiant remains of Christian Saxons, possible of the seventh century, who died in defence of their Lewes settlement.

The tiny toll-gate cottages of the turnpike era are still scattered everywhere along the roads leading out of Lewes. There is one on the road leading into Ringmer, where also the Glyndebourne Road corner is still known locally as Paygate. There is one on the road to Uckfield and one at the village of Offham. A round toll-booth also still stands at the Brighton end of the Lewes By-pass.

The better north to south roads certainly succeeded in opening up the County to traffic from London. Coaches now ran from the Capital to the coast on Mondays, Wednesdays and Fridays, taking about seven hours for the single journey. In the 1830's a total of thirty six coaches altogether were employed on the London to Brighton road, needing a grand total of 1,200 horses en route.

Easier travel also encouraged more local visiting from town to town. From the diary of a Horsham gentleman, for instance, a Mr. John Baker writing in 1776: "I rode over the finest turnpike road that can be got, to the Star at Lewes before two . . ." He then dined and visited his local friends to hear all the latest gossip . . . "Just heard the old Duchess Newcastle is dead and came away at half past six and to Brighton in an hour and a quarter to Ship. Ball night there. I go to Coffee Room. Read papers . . ." A day in the life of a now-travelling Georgian worthy.

More traffic along the roads unfortunately encouraged more highwaymen, who converged, like vultures, where the pickings were the greatest. For a time they were a successful menace. But eventually the thickets and scrub that lined the improved roads along the loneliest stretches were cleared and the "gentlemen of the roads" were finally either caught or persuaded into some alternative line of roguery. If they were caught they were given short shrift: "My servant Will went to Norwich this morning to see three highwaymen hung . . ." (written in 1777). They then swung on the creaking gibbets until their bones had been picked clean by weathering and predators.

Lewes and The Prince Regent

Coincidentally with the improvement in travel came the advertisements, already mentioned, of Dr. Russell of the healthy properties of sea water. When he first built his house for treatments in Brighthelmstone in 1754, he had found it an insignificant fishing port of around 2,000 people. By 1821 it was a large town of nearly 25,000 people.

This phenomenal growth was greatly, though not entirely, due to its poularity as a health resort. For in addition to this in 1783, the Prince of Wales made his first visit to the town and was enchanted. His subsequent Pavilion became the centre of fashion. The popularity of the town, as Brighton, grew by leaps and bounds and gracious terraces in Regency style, spread along the sea front from the Royal Crescent to Brunswick Square.

The Regent, with his passion for horses, also had built the royal stables and the riding-school (now the Corn Exchange and the Dome) alongside his seaside palace. But Brighton at that time had no-race-course and so the Prince turned eastwards, whipping his coach and six along the new turnpike road, past Stanmer Park and Falmer village, to the racecourse which had been long established on the Downs outside Lewes.

Lewes Races, since the reign of Queen Anne, had been held as a two-day meeting. It now became a seven-day event and was held at the beginning of August. The climax of the week was the running of the King's Plate sponsored, in his day, by the Duke of Newcastle. The crowds flocked in from surrounding Sussex. The nobles came in their carriages from which they viewed the races until a grandstand was erected, by public subscription, in 1772. The ordinary folk came in on horseback or on foot.

There were the inevitable additions to the occasion, the tipsters, the booths, the gypsies and the pitched battles which had "long been practised". The eighteenth century writer sounds sadly philosophical! The King's Plate brought in a prize of a hundred guineas and was run, in 1763, in eight minutes twenty five seconds. That was a memorable day for a Mr. Turner who came in from his general store at East Hoathly and wrote vividly about it in his diary:- "Came home about three o'clock (in the morning!) and how happy should I be if I could say, sober . . ." At least his horse would have steadily plodded his familiar way home in safety, whatever the state of the rider.

When the races were finished for the day, the crowds pushed their way down to the favourite racing inns at the top fo the town, the Running Horse, the Black Horse and the Pelham Arms, the latter still popular public houses. There they spent the evening drinking, arguing and singing.

For the fashionable, there were balls and dinners in the big houses, Pelham House, the Grange, the Friars and, for the public in general, at the Star and the White Hart. The Prince, resplendent in the uniform of the Dragoons, would dine with his friend Ferdinando Poole at the House of the Grey Friars along Friars Walk. Ferdinando was, "One of the best patrons and staunchest supporters of the turf". Or he would visit William Newton at the Grange, a colonel in the Prince's own regiment of the Light Dragoons. If he did drive his coach and four down cobbled Keere Street, as local legend insists, at least there is a plaque commemorating the feat at the foot of the hill.

Lewes became almost as fashionable, in its quieter way, as the Prince's Brighton. In 1771 Prince Ernest of Mecklenberg-Strelitz, a relation of the Queen, wrote ". . . liked the town so well that he would like to live here." The Prince's brother, the Duke of Cumberland, was also a visitor, while when the scandal-monger John Wilkes and his daughter came, in 1770, they almost caused a riot.

The racecourse saw its last meeting in 1964, but the grandstand buildings still silhouette against the sky above the old Lewes Battle-ground. It made Lewes a great centre for blood-stock breeding. As recently as 1980 there were still five important racing stables hidden among the back roads of the town together with three farriers, and the early morning rush-hour traffic along Nevill Road was invariably held up by strings of elegant racers crossing to exercise on the Downs.

Now there is just one racing stable, on the Downs behind the prison. But Lewes still has racing and betting skills coursing through her veins. Many are the shopkeepers who will still lay a bet for you or give you the "cert for the day" at Brighton, Plumpton, Goodwood or Lingfield.

The memorial to the Finnish prisoners of war from the Russian Army of the Crimean War in the churchyard of St. John-sub-Castro.

The Napoleonic Wars

By the end of the 18th century the horses of Sussex were being commandeered for more hazardous sport. Revolutionary France had burst its frontiers and, under the power-hungry Napoleon Bonaparte, was threatening the stability of the whole of the Western World.

Lewes, as in earlier days, was again in the forefront of the battle line and the whole of Sussex around became a prime defence area. Military personnel and armaments were drafted into the County in their thousands. Local militia were organised into voluntary units of "Home Guard" forces.

The drafted soldiers from elsewhere were 'furriners'. Despite the increased trade that they brought they were not welcomed either in the villages or in the towns such as Lewes. Barracks were eventually built for their lodgings, the weather-boarded Hunt Kennels House at Ringmer being originally one such barracks. Lewes and the people of the surrounding countryside had their own personal tragedies during this, and the succeeding wars of the 19th and 20th centuries. A most poignant memorial to the losses of just one family can be found in the plain, Norman chancel of the little church at Hamsey, scarcely a mile up the Ouse from Cliffe Bridge.

Here the wall plaques tell their own story:-
Captain John Shiffner, killed at Sebastopol, 1855, aged 31.
Sir John Shiffner, R.A., saw service in the Zulu War.
Sir John Bridger Shiffner, Royal Sussex Regiment, killed in action in 1918, aged 19.
Sir Henry Burrows Shiffner (brother of Sir John) Royal Artillery, killed in the Desert War, 1941.

The Bridgers and, following them by marriage, the Shiffners lived at Coombe Place, Offham and were patrons of the Parish of Hamsey in St. John Without, Lewes.

During the Napoleonic Wars the prison on North Street was used to accommodate prisoners of war. In the Lewes Gallery of the Sussex Archaeological Museum is a large model of a galleon fashioned by the French prisoners from meat bones.

Again, in the Crimean War of the mid-nineteenth century (1854-1856), Lewes saw yet more trails of unhappy prisoners of war driven up its streets. These were Russian soldiers, mainly from Finland. Work by them is also displayed in the town, this time fashioned in wood. The gaol of North Street was, by this time, not in general use as a town prison, as the present Lewes Gaol, along the road to Brighton, had been built and opened in 1856.

The unfortunate Finnish prisoners from the army of Imperial Russia are commemorated in a memorial in the churchyard of St. John-sub-castro. It is well worth a visit to see this imposing monument that towers marvellously above the long grass and tilting gravestones. The memorial is to twenty-one of their number who died during their captivity and was built on the personal orders of the Tsar Alexander II in 1877. It was later restored by the Communist Government of the USSR in 1957.

Despite the unhappy consequence that twenty-one of their company died in captivity, the prisoners had been treated well in Lewes and they were impressed with the kindness of the Lewes folk. Their feelings were expressed in a most agreeable letter of thanks to the Senior Constable of Lewes on their repatriation at the end of the war. A Russian gun, captured during the war, was subsequently placed in the grounds of the Castle in Lewes, as a memento, where it still stands.

The harshest effects of the Napoleonic War were felt by the poorer, country folk of the Sussex countryside. Downland had been ploughed up and pockets of waste land brought into cultivation, but the bad harvest of 1799 brought the century to a close, in the countryside, with agricultural upheaval, bitterness and riots. The wage of the farm-worker which averaged 12 to 15 shillings, stayed static and the inept handling of the situation by all the authorities led directly on to the growth of theft, rioting and general disturbances that followed the ending of the war in 1815.

But Lewes Town was not so adversely affected. With wool being in supreme demand for uniforms, and food being at a premium, her trade flourished and her townsfolk profited. Napoleon's sneering gibe of England as merely being "A nation of shopkeepers", was well and profitably manifested in Lewes. Her people were good responsible merchant folk who drew an honest - bar the smuggling - living from the countryside around them and helped each other along as best they could.

Civic Generosity and the Growth of Libraries

Again, as it was so remarkable in earlier times, it is astonishing to read, today, of how many gifts and grants were made to the less fortunate in the town by those in easier circumstances. It seems to have been an inherent tradition of the English way of life through history and no more so than in Lewes during the later centuries.

The townsfolk were continually giving money for the destitute, money for the hospitals, money for coal for the poor etc., etc. In their wills they left land and rents to be used for poor relief. They bought up stretches of land and gave them to the town for the use of all. They made gifts of plate to the municipality as well as to the churches. In 1742 the pest-house had been built by public contributions, and even the fire-engines were provided through public gift and subscription in 1726 and 1784.

In Medieval and Tudor times money had been set aside for the training of the town apprentices. In the 18th century the gifts took the form of libraries of books. A library of 532 volumes was left to the borough by a resident clergyman in 1720, with money added to buy even more books. A Library Society was set up in 1785, which included a vast 10,000 volumes according to account. It was not a free institution, the annual subscription for the ninety-three members being £1-5s.

In the mid-nineteenth century, 1862, the Fitzroy Memorial Library was provided for the town by the daughter of Baron Rothschild, in memory of her husband, Henry Fitzroy M.P. for Lewes before his death in 1859. Built in the red-brick and ornate style of the Victorian Gothick, it stands quaintly in Georgian Lewes on the corner of Cliffe High Street and Friars Walk. Its contents were later moved to the School of Art, a similarly elaborate Gothick building in 1874. This is now the Lewes Public Library standing on the corner of Albion Street.

Nonconformity

Lastly, a striking feature of 18th century Lewes was the further development of the Evangelical Movement and the widespread building of the many chapels to accommodate the different sects.

During this time, the Established Church of England was becoming "formal, pedestrian and prosaic", in a word, complacent. Many of the Evangelical sects had also lost a good deal of their initial fighting enthusiasm. The latter half of the century presented a very different picture and an upsurge of religious revival that can largely be attributed to the exhortations of John Wesley and his followers.

Wesley began his influential, countryside preaching in 1738. His visits to Sussex were mainly between 1758 and 1790 and his last sermon in 1791 was said to have been given outside the wall of the parish church of Winchelsea.

In actual conversions, he had, by his own admission, few countable successes in the County. Perhaps he was preaching to the converted and the rest were too worldly? His own comments may provide a clue. In 1773 he wrote in his diary, "I found the people (of Rye) willing to hear the good word . . . But they will not part with the accursed smuggling"! However his overall influence was as crucial in reviving Church and Chapel interest, discipline and growth here as it was everywhere else.

In Lewes, this surge of renewed religious enthusiasm gave rise to yet another sect, the new Independents, established by that intriguing lady, Selina, Countess of Huntington (1709-1791). Inspired directly by the preaching of Wesley which was directed towards the poorer and non-churchgoing people, her aim was to bring revival to the peoples of her own, wealthier class.

The first of her chapels in Sussex was next door to one of her own houses in Brighton in 1761. But in 1775 she built an Independent Chapel on the old Bostal in the Cliffe in Lewes. This was a foundation of Calvinist persuasion allied to Methodism. Only a trace of it remains, a few doors up from the foot of the hill on the left-hand side. But it still gives its name to the lane, Chapel Hill.

In time, a larger off-shoot from this chapel was built as the Jireh Chapel (1805) which still stands, close to the Cuilfail tunnel. It was fortunate, one feels, not to have been swallowed up altogether by the tunnel as, in the road alterations, it lost its peaceful green surround of grass and trees and now stands, stark and lonely, surrounded by 20th century traffic on all sides. In its time it was supported by a huge congregation and also housed four hundred young worshippers in the adjacent Sunday School building which was almost ruined in the hurricane of 1987.

This chapel contains the tomb of that equally interesting character, William Huntington - no relation to the Countess - the converted coal-heaver with the silver tongue who insisted on adding "S.S." to his name to signify "Sinner Saved". His ouput of sermons and books was prodigious. As flamboyant in death as he was in life, he died in 1813 in Tunbridge Wells, by which time he had himself married into the aristocracy, and his body was born, in a hearse drawn by six black-plumed horses, all the way back from Tunbridge Wells to Lewes for burial. His hearse is said to have been followed by a mourning procession a mile long.

The still picturesque and thriving chapel at Golden Cross, along the road from Lewes to Hailsham, was also an offshoot of that on Chapel Hill. This was built in 1813 and was served until well into this present century by preachers who travelled manfully out of Lewes on horse-back, and later by bicycle, staying the night in the tiny, primitive room adjoining the tile-hung chapel.

Through the 18th and 19th centuries the other non-conformist sects in the town moved from one premises to another as their congregations and their fortunes increased. In 1785 a Baptist congregation moved to a new chapel in Foundry Lane, Cliffe, when the new Friends Meeting House was built in Friars Walk. In Eastport Lane, Southover, the "Old Meeting House" was built, again for a Baptist gathering. It is now an attractive private town cottage. The large Eastgate Baptist Chapel was sited at the foot of Eastgate Street in 1819, rebuilt in 1843, where it still remains.

The Methodists, as a sect separated from the Established Church, finally did penetrate Lewes, building their first chapel in 1807 and rebuilding it in 1867 in Station Street. It is now a chapel no more and houses a pine-furniture centre.

In Market Street, the former Presbyterian Chapel, built in 1865, is now a small factory. In Little East Street the chapel has become an interesting conversion to flats.

The most imposing chapel building of all was undoubtedly the Independent Congregational Tabernacle in what is now the High Street Precinct opposite Dial House, which was built in 1816. Now a row of graceless shops, it was rebuilt in 1832 with a classic pillared facade fine enough to have enhanced a site in the City of London. It contained seating for twelve hundred worshippers, while its Sunday School building, on the site of the Etna Iron Works in Railway Lane, housed another five-hundred children. Victorian Lewes indeed had her grander moments of architecture.

Another such impressive portico, which could well be mistaken for a previous chapel facade, is now the entrance to the agricultural firm of Culverwells off Malling Street. In fact, to move from the sublime to the mundane, it was originally the entrance to a brewery.

The conversion of the back of Henry Goring's house at the Westgate, in 1700, still remains a chapel to this day. The entrance is down a narrow path from the High Street alongside the Bull House. It has now passed to the Unitarian persuasion who share their premises with the Methodists and many others.

At the same time, the Anglican Church was also much revived by the exhortations of the Wesleys. Much of St. Michael's Church, in the High Street, was rebuilt in 1755. All Saints Church was rebuilt in 1806/7 and the Church of St. John-sub-castro was re-erected entirely in 1838.

Finally, the Roman Catholics were at last permitted to build and open their church of The Sacred Heart in St. Anne's Parish in 1870. However, feelings still ran high and it is said to have caused much indignation and opposition, particularly at the nearby Pelham Arms which was one of the Bonfire Society bases at the time.

XI. LEWES IN THE NINETEENTH CENTURY

The Georgian England of the Age of Reason retained its elegant Georgian quality, in Lewes, until well into the 19th century.

Although France had declared war against England in 1793, Napoleon was largely concerned in dominating the European mainland until the turn of the century. Even when invasion then threatened, it threatened a countryside in the south-east still rural and outwardly stable in spite of rising prices and growing agricultural problems.

The clubs of Lewes were still filled with be-wigged gentlemen, in their knee breeches and full-skirted coats, their three-cornered hats bobbing to their owners' hot-headed arguments. In the streets, the incoming farmer or farm labourer was conspicuous for his home-spun, heavy smock. Gallant soldiers in their brilliant red coats enlivened the scene among the carriages of the wealthy, the carts and waggons of the rustics, and the mail-coach swinging into the yard of the Star Inn with an exciting flourish of music from its horns.

Even as late as 1822, when William Cobbett came to Lewes on one of his famous "Rural Rides", he describes the town in lines that invoke a very familiar "Quality Street" atmosphere:- "There is a great extent of rich meadows above and below Lewes. The town itself is a model of solidity and neatness. The buildings are substantial to the very outskirts; the pavement good and complete; the shops nice and clean; the people well-dressed; and, though last but not least, the girls remarkably pretty, as indeed they are in most parts of Sussex; round faces, features small, little hands and wrists, plump arms and bright eyes.

The Sussex men, too, are remarkable for their good looks. A Mr. Baxter, a stationer at Lewes, showed me a farmer's account book which is a very complete thing of its kind.

The inns are good at Lewes, the people civil not servile, and the charges really (considering the taxes) far below what one could reasonably expect."

River-trade and Industry

Economically, as has been seen, Lewes itself prospered while the hostilities with France lasted. Even the iron industry revived and the iron works near Cliffe Bridge was producing ordnance in the Napoleonic War just as, in the First World War a century later, the Phoenix Ironworks was to prosper.

Under the always energetic First Lord Sheffield big improvements were made along the Ouse. Canals were cut and locks built to maintain a navigable waterway from Newhaven to Lindfield (Upper Ryland Bridge). The work took the whole of the war years to complete and comprised eighteen locks with cut-offs to Shortbridge and to the Offham chalk-pit.

In 1801 there were twenty-seven barges based at Lewes Quay. These were hauled by horses from the tow-paths, although some could raise sail. As a direct result, four paper mills developed upstream from Lewes over the next fifty years, the first being sited at the Pells.

The trade up-river included chalk, lime and stone for road making according to the methods of the new road makers, Telford and Macadam. Foodstuffs and timber were also hauled. The trade downstream included corn, chalk and lime, paper, wool and iron goods.

It was the coming of the railways, in the mid-nineteenth century, that put an end to the river trading. Ironically the last heavy up-stream cargoes were the bricks that built the huge railway viaduct on the Brighton Line north of Brighton and Haywards Heath. It was a climax in the long industrial revolution that had been gathering momentum over so many years in England.

From this time onwards, Lewes, like the rest of England, was to face immense changes both outwardly, along her streets, and inwardly in every sphere of life, social, economic and political. It was the beginning of the seemingly catastrophic changes of the Victorian Age that finally catapulted the whole world, and Lewes along with it, into that explosion of modern culture, technical achievement and internationalism which is the stamp of the twentieth century.

The Coming of the Railways

Between 1845 and 1858 the railways came to Lewes. In 1841 the line had been laid down between London and Brighton. In 1846 this was now extended from Brighton into Lewes. Nineteen days later, June 27th, track was opened linking Lewes to St. Leonards. The railway from Lewes to Keymer followed in 1847, that to Newhaven in the same year. This was extended to Seaford in 1846. A further line to the north, to Uckfield and Tunbridge Wells, was opened in 1868 and a branch off to Sheffield Park and East Grinstead in 1882.

Symbolic perhaps of the crushing determination of the railways to stamp their mark upon Lewes, as everywhere else, was their siting of the first railway station and its goods yard. These were laid out, in 1846, over part of the site of the Friars. The Friars, itself a reminder of the days long ago when the Greyfriars (Friars Minor) of the Franciscan Order busied themselves mightily to bring enlightenment and healing to the townsfolk of Mediaeval Lewes.

The station building was embellished, in true Victorian style, with pilasters and brickwork. This was closed in 1857, the Goods Station being retained, and a junction station built just north of the present station. In 1889 this subsequently gave way to the present railway station in Station Road where all the lines now join. The line to Uckfield was shortsightedly closed during the 'Beeching' era in very recent times. That at Sheffield Park is now the 'Bluebell Line'. All the others are still in good order.

The railways were financed by wealthy investors, in three different companies, just as the turnpike roads had been before them. Labour was plentiful, skills already learned in road and canal making being well utilised. In the Lewes area, as in many other spheres, the wealthy investors were, as often as not, those

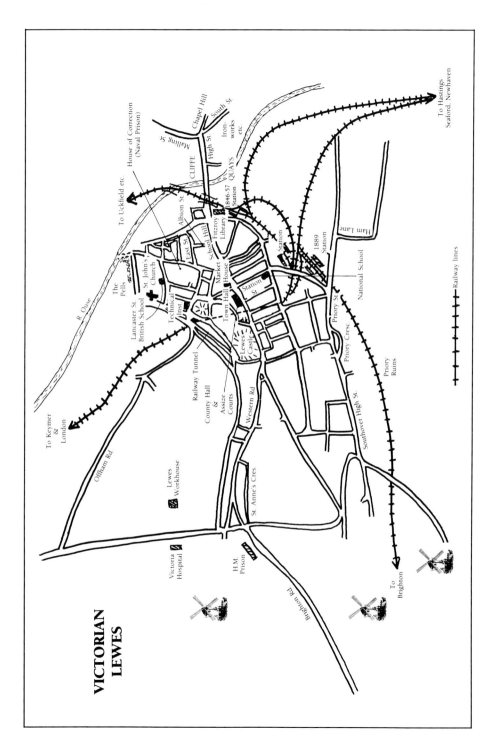

VICTORIAN LEWES

To Hastings
Seaford, Newhaven

Chapel Hill

South St.

Malling St.

High St.

Iron-
works
etc.

House of Correction
(Naval Prison)

CLIFFE

QUAYS

To Uckfield etc.

1846-57
Station

Albion St.

School Hill

Fitzroy
Library

Station

1889
Station

Ham Lane

National School

The Pells

St. John's
Church

East St.

Market

Station
St.

Priory St.

R. Ouse

Lancaster St.
British School

Technical
Inst.

Town Hall House

Lewes
Castle

Priory Cresc.

Priory
Ruins

Railway lines

County Hall
&
Assize
Courts

Railway Tunnel

Western Rd

Southover High St.

To Keymer
&
London

Offham Rd

Lewes
Workhouse

St. Anne's Cres.

Victoria
Hospital

H.M. Prison

Brighton Rd

To Brighton

successful Dissenting merchants of which Lewes always had her full quota. It is interesting to note, incidentally, that the Bradshaw Railway Guide was also the product of a Quaker, a Mr. Bradshaw.

Looking at the map of Lewes of the early 19th century, and superimposing upon it the tentacles spread of the railway network that tightened its hold upon the town in the short space of twelve years between 1846 and 1858, one is left wondering how old Lewes managed to survive at all. Quite obviously nothing could withstand the vigour and the ingenuity of the Victorian railway engineer.

It has already been told how the railway navvies carved the deep cutting right through the Priory ruins and, to the astonishment of all, resurrected the bones of the Priory founder and foundress, the Lord and Lady de Warenne, for more reverent reburial in the church of St. John in Southover.

After demolishing the Georgian Friars mansion, they then flung an iron bridge over the lower High Street, in 1858, which was later replaced by a brick built span, that took the steam trains thundering and belching over the heads of banks, shops and shoppers alike for the rest of the century and until the 1960s.

Perhaps it was fortunate that the castle stood too high, on its lofty motte, for even the most philistine of engineers to destroy it. Undeterred, they bored straight underneath it, from south to north, through the soft chalk of the Lewes spur, to direct their line towards London. It can be seen emerging alongside the hidden cul-de-sac of Talbot Terrace which is reached by a steep flight of steps from White Hill, along the Offham Road.

But offering faster and cheaper transport, as they did, it must be conceded that the railways gave an invaluable impetus to industry in Lewes, particularly in the already industrial Cliffe area. Here there were three iron foundries, one ship-building yard, two tanneries and timber yards. Three corn-merchants flourished, and the warehouses of Stricklands and Stevensons, slate-hung in red brick, still stand along the riverside. Moreover, to provide for her seventy public houses there were seven breweries in the town by the mid-nineteenth century. Harveys, built in 1790 north of Cliffe Bridge, is the only one to survive today.

Nearer to Lewes town centre was the inevitable candle factory supplying much of the lighting in these days before gas and electricity. This has recently been well developed into a shopping precinct behind Market Street. There were other smaller craft-works for the necessities of life and small luxuries. Pipe Passage commemorates the clay-pipe maker on the site. Another interesting and long-gone craft was the manufacture of "Large green umbrellas on their cane frames" for the shepherds of Sussex, for which Lewes was noted in Victorian times. Another, cutlery, is remembered by English Passage, off the Cliffe, named after the English family who were cutlers here at the turn of the 19th century.

The Cliffe

The Cliffe, like Southover, has always been a part of Lewes to maintain its own character. Very much the quayside area of the town, it was always subject to flooding until recent times and was notoriously swampy and unhealthy. In 1671, "The water was so high in the Cliffe that men waded up to their middle by the brig". In 1772 they cheerfully floated around the street in boats!

The main street of the Cliffe itself had always been far too narrow for all the traffic that used it. In 1829 the south side was pulled down, and set back, as far east as Morris Road, named after Ebenezer Morris, 1801-88, who owned the Lewes Foundry here. At the end of Morris Road, until the coming of North Sea Gas, stood the gasworks. Lewes was lit by gas from 1822 when the Lewes Gas Light Company was established. The Waterworks was built in 1833. Electricity did not arrive until 1901.

In Medieval times, the parish well had stood in the centre of the main road by St. Thomas' Church, just as it had at the top of School Hill for the centre of Lewes. The parish pump of 1830 still stands alongside the church wall. Here too, behind the church, were held the Cliffe sheep and cattle fairs and the Wednesday market. The removal of these elsewhere by 1753 "Gave much umbrage to the inhabitants". The sheep fair, in October, was moved to "Henry Shelley's Field", now Baxter's Field, in 1747.

The Cliffe was always an area of very decided and independent opinions and, in the later centuries, particularly non-conformist. Even into modern times, it was in no small part due to the spirited defence of South Street residents to preserve their street intact that persuaded the 20th century planners to thrust their remarkable tunnel right through the backing chalk hill to bring the by-pass traffic into the town and over the new Phoenix Causeway.

South Street in years past had been a road of many ale-houses, rope-makers, chandlers and timberyards that served the quayside fraternity of the Cliffe. The Lewes Boating Club now replaces, fittingly, the boat-repair yard of mid-Victorian times and before. Near it the sign of "The Barge Master's House" brings back yet another memory of the thriving river trade of old.

Near the end of the street, the Snowdrop Inn still stands witness to the doleful winter's night in December 1836, when an avalanche of snow, from the high face of the Downs behind it, engulfed eight Lewes folk who "refused to be druv" out of their homes in the middle of the night and so, alas, perished in their beds.

The Cliffe Church, dedicated to St. Thomas a Becket, was probably a foundation of the Archbishop of Canterbury's monastery at Malling. As its dedication indicates, it was built at the end of the 12th century after the murder of Becket by the knights of Henry II. Legend has it that the guilty knights fled from Canterbury to Malling after the murder.

As has been mentioned earlier, the church contains an interesting copy of the Charter of Henry IV of 1409 granting Market Rights to the Cliffe and the right to hold two fairs annually on the Feasts of St. Matthew and St. Mark. There is also the comparatively rare coat of arms of Queen Elizabeth I dated 1598.

Agricultural Unrest in the Lewes Countryside

In the first three decades of the 19th century trade and industry continued the prosperity of Lewes, but in the surrounding agricultural area conditions deteriorated considerably. Before, and through, the Napoleonic War profits went to the wealthy landowners and the self-employed farmers. The rich became richer but the poor became poorer. For tenant farmers rents were raised to match the post-war rising cost of living and the bond between the large landowner and his tenant became looser and less sympathetic. Fixed wages and post war unemployment drove the small farmer and the farm worker to starvation level.

The central government hoped to keep unrest stifled by insisting on each parish supplementing the low agricultural wages by poor-law hand outs in cash or kind. It was a huge burden on each locality. Sussex had the highest poor-rates in England. In 1844, one thousand two hundred and sixty-eight people received relief. Ever concerned, old John Ellman, the farmer from Glynde, said with great pessimism, "I consider the distress of the farmers so great that nothing can be done to save many from absolute ruin".

Although Sussex folk were too rooted in their own stubborn soil to be carried away to the extremes of violence encountered in other parts of Britain, riots flared up in the vicinity of Lewes. Hayricks were set on fire, sheep were stolen and windows smashed. In 1835, thirty men of Ringmer set on an officer of the Chailey Union to demand higher wages and cash relief. In November 1830, Lord Gage met with several hundreds of the rioters in Ringmer to hear their grievances, while Lord Chichester (the current Pelham) assisted three hundred people to emigrate to the growing colonies in Canada, Australia and New Zealand.

But the Winter Assizes in Lewes in 1830 took a less merciful view of the trouble makers. Fifty men and women came up for trial. One was executed, sixteen jailed and seventeen transported to the Australian convict settlement of Botany Bay. Eighteen were happily acquitted.

As soon as the Act forbidding people to band together for protest was repealed in 1824, Lewes led the way in initiating Labourers Trade Unions to meet regularly in the town as they also did in Uckfield and Seaford. These kept up the pressure for higher wages. Eventually things improved. The Corn Laws were repealed in 1846, overseas markets built up again and more employment was provided in growing local industries. By 1846 the biggest employers in the area had already come to be the railways.

Fortunately, the Test and Corporation Acts of 1828 had, at last, given freedom to the non-conformists to take part in public life and administration which, in Lewes particularly, stimulated much better local government all round.

Finally, during the last half of the century, the Poor Rates system was overhauled. Instead of the burden for poor relief resting on the shoulders of each parish it was now amalgamated. Huge workhouses replaced the small, separate poor-houses of each parish. Many of these latter remain today, now picturesque private cottages. There is a delightful cottage on Castle Banks still retaining its name of "The Old Poor House" and St. Michael's Court, in Keere Street, is an attractive flint building, up against the old town wall, rebuilt as parish alms-houses on a site given by Thomas Matthew in 1690 for the housing of poor widows.

The huge Victorian workhouse in South Chailey, which later became the Pouchlands Hospital (now closed), was a fine institution, it had provided home and board for many hundreds in its life. The Lewes workhouse stood on the site of the present De Montfort Flats. Built in 1868, it was pulled down in 1960. This too, through the years, had given house and home to two hundred and fifty poor people constantly through its century of use. The workhouse system was finally abolished in 1929 and the workhouses gradually phased out over the next ten years.

In the mid-19th century the population of rural Sussex declined, partly through emigration as the colonies developed and partly through a shift townwards. Prices fell and wages went a little farther even for the poorest. In Lewes itself, the population of 1801 had doubled by 1851, to 9,000 people. But only another 2,000 were added by 1900. It is now between 14,000 and 16,000.

Rural troubles petered out as agricultural prosperity temporarily took an upward swing. The Bonfire Boys of Lewes had the last say.

In 1847 the celebrations reached a fever-pitch of excitement and hostility to all and sundry. The evening turned into a pitched battle in the streets. The local defence troops were called out and the newly-formed Metropolitan Police, all one hundred of them, charged into the fray. With great solemnity Lord Chichester read The Riot Act from the steps of the County Hall and instituted an immediate curfew and the threat of penalty for treason.

But it was the final explosion of the turbulent times. The following year the level headed townsfolk organised the Bonfire Societies to regulate Bonfire Night from then on. There was still a cheerful tendency to "throw alarming bangers" through the crowded streets and prudent shopkeepers shuttered their windows by mid-afternoon (as they still do) on November 5th, but today the Societies are a highly respected section of Lewes and their celebrations are a public spirited magnificence seen nowhere else in the Country.

The Royal Visit

Life was far from being all riot and discontent in Lewes, however, in the nineteenth century. The town took an active interest in national affairs as opposed to its own swings of fortune. It had celebrated the war victories, Trafalgar and Waterloo, with "Banners and bonfires" in traditional local style.

In 1820 the old King George III finally melted from his twilight world into the grave. Although Lewes had been so popular with the Prince of Wales in his Regency days, it shared the general public outcry at his high handed treatment of Queen Caroline and published its own indignant outrage at his behaviour.

But it gave a royal welcome to the next sovereign, William IV and his queen Adelaide when they graced Lewes with a personal state visit just after their accession in October 1830.

They came to the Friars, formerly "the Grey Friars", the house sited on the Medieval Friary that had been acquired by John Kyme M.P. after the Dissolution of the monasteries. Rebuilt as a Georgian mansion in the 18th century, Mr Nehemiah Wimble, a wealthy non-conformist, was then the owner. It was a grand occasion. A great banquet was prepared in the mansion and a fine armorial dinner-service, in Worcester china, made to commemorate the event. It is one of the treasures still to be seen in the Anne of Cleves House in Southover.

Dr. Gideon Mantell has left us a vivid description of the occasion. The King came often to the Pavilion, the palace built by his brother when Regent, in Brighton. In October 1830 he rode over from there in his carriage at 12.30 pm to enter Lewes by the Western Road. The streets were gay with flags and streamers and the houses all decorated with greenery and flowers. Everybody was there to welcome the first official visit of the Sovereign to Lewes since the Middle Ages.

The school children formed the first welcoming party but the infants had been thoughtfully hoisted clear of the crowds into St. Anne's churchyard where they no doubt had the best view of all. It was a lovely sunny day and the royal carriage was cheered lustily the length of the high road to the foot of School Hill and along Friars Walk to the door of the Friars.

The royal standard flew from the County Hall, the Market Tower, the Friars and two of the churches and cannon roared from Brack Mount and Cliffe Hill. After the banquet, which included the presence of the Shelley family, the ladies of whom held places at Court, the cavalcade drove back up School Hill, the King to be further entertained at the new Council Offices (now the County Courts) and the Queen to climb the Castle mound and be shown the view of the countryside and the decorated town.

A copy of the Rev. T. W. Horsefield's "History of Lewes" was presented to the King and a silver goblet was purchased by the town to add to its civic treasures to commemorate the occasion.

There was no time for the King and Queen to be shown the Geological museum of Dr. Mantell, as hoped. Perhaps it was just as well, his majesty was a good and kind man, but no academic. The collection is now in the British Museum. The cavalcade reformed and the royal cortege was back in Brighton by five of the afternoon. A most enjoyable and successful day . . .

Dr. Mantell comments on how well conducted was every part of the proceedings with "No military in evidence anywhere". And how typical of Lewes to organise such a happy and successful handling of enormous crowds to everybody's good natured enjoyment.

Queen Victoria never made an official visit to the town in all her long reign, although she did once pass through. Lewes had heralded her coronation with an enormous party on the Dripping Pan, on June 28th 1838, where hundreds of the poor of Lewes and Southover were treated to a "Substantial dinner" by public subscription in the presence of all the magistrates and the clergy of the town. How patronising it sounds to our modern ears, though no doubt it was well intentioned and enjoyed by all. The occasion was rounded off, in the evening, by the expected fireworks. Her Golden Jubilee, too, was celebrated in fine style, the streets being said to have been filled with the massed hundreds of the Sunday School children from all the churches and chapels of the town.

Schools and Sunday Schools

School children and Sunday School children have figured in the forgoing chronicles of public events. The Sunday School movement began at the end of the 18th century when Robert Raikes of Gloucester arranged accommodation and teaching, from his own purse, for the unlettered children of Gloucester. These had been pressed into factory work at a horrifyingly early age all week, and were out prowling the streets unkempt and uncared for all Sunday.

His aims at first were simple, to keep them off the streets, to teach them to read the Bible, and to encourage them in the elementary disciplines of combing their hair (combs were given as prizes) and washing their hands and faces.

But the movement met a real need and spread like wildfire through every town in the Country. It was then taken up, by the chapels and churches. In Lewes, Sunday Schools numbered their children in hundreds and these had to be accommodated in separate halls erected specially for the purpose. Notable, among others, that in Railway Lane and alongside the Jireh Chapel are still standing though no longer put to their original use.

Secular education on any noteworthy scale in Lewes is first recorded in the founding of the Free Grammar School, for boys only, by Mrs Agnes Morley, of the Grange, in Eastport Lane in Southover in 1512. By public gift, the school was moved to St. Anne's Parish where, mercifully, the schoolmaster was also provided with a house nearby, for he had become "Quite unequal to the task of breasting Keere Hill twice a day"! The Old Grammar School, as it is now called, latterly incorporating the Lewes High School for Girls, is still a thriving and respected private school for both boys and girls.

Through the later centuries there were a great many small private schools around the town that all served their turn for a limited time. John Evelyn, the diarist, and a member of the Royal Society in later life, attended one run by a Mr Potts in the Cliffe. As time went on, the private schools provided education for both boys and girls. Of particular note, in 1794, was Mr John Button's Academy at Wells Croft in St. Anne's parish, "A very good seminary".

It is at this time that the roots of our modern education system are to be found. In 1808, Joseph Lancaster, a Quaker philanthropist of London, founded the Lancastrian Society to profide daily schooling, on a strictly non-denominational basis, for as many children as possible. He organised his schools on the economical system of the older "pupil-teachers" teaching the younger ones. The idea spread rapidly. The schools came to be known as "British Schools" when the Lancastrian Society later became the British and Foreign School Society.

It is a tribute to the forward looking attitude of Lewes at that time, that her first British School was founded here only one year later, in 1809. It was known as "The Octagonal School" from its shape, and it stood in Lancaster Street, the name of which still commemorates Joseph Lancaster, near the site of the Lewes Little Theatre. It provided a good basic education for two to three hundred boys and girls and was a milestone in general education in the town.

During the 19th century, the Church of England, spurred by these non-conformist efforts, formed the "National Society" in 1811, to "Educate the poor in the principles of the Established Church". The buildings of their Central National School in Lewes still stands at the bottom of Station Street. It was founded in 1843 to educate three hundred and seventy five boys and girls, and the two life size figures of children that originally embellished its frontage can still be seen in All Saints Church. In brick and flint, it is one of the most pleasing of the Victorian buildings of the town. The St. Anne's National School stood at the corner of De Montfort Road and is now still used educationally as part of the Lewes Tertiary College.

Later in the 19th and 20th centuries, came the larger Private and Public schools such as Battle Abbey in 1847, Brighton College in 1848, Roedean in 1898 and the Southover Manor School in Lewes itself. The Acts of 1870 and 1902 introduced free state schooling, and led to the formation of the many State Primary schools and the Free State Grammar School of the town, which has become the Priory Comprehensive School and the Tertiary College.

Housing Expansion

During the 19th century, Lewes became much enlarged in size. Initially, with the population steadily rising since 1790, Lewes had been hard put to it to find room for so many more people. Centrally, it expanded by building "New Town". This is the area of housing that now covers the north-east section of the spur slope, which was laid out into a series of neat, terraced roads that swung from School Hill round to the new Offham Road. The Offham Road had been cut along the lower side of the hill to give an alternative access in from the London Road to the bottom of the town.

The little town cottages of Sun Street (1810) and St. John's Street were built with a variety of brick and mathematical tiling or with weatherboard facings. Mount Pleasant followed in 1826. East Street, with its pleasant bayed windows and inset doorways was built in 1793 and Albion Street, with its interesting cast iron balconies, was cut through from School Hill to join it in 1822.

The Elephant and Castle was built in 1838, by which time this small corner of the town had improved greatly. Now called Commercial Square, it became a thriving trading corner of the town.

The small theatre (1789) which stood here closed down in 1825 after only thirty years running. The present Lewes Little Theatre, which is its thriving successor in the present century, stands in Lancaster Street, only two roads away, and, in typical Lewes fashion, is a theatre run by the people and for the people, being an amateur theatre of professional quality.

On the site of the old theatre (and the present police station) rose the new Mechanics Institute. Built in 1825, it was a sign of this age when education for all was suddenly becoming valued and British engineers and engineering were leading the World in the Industrial Revolution.

Mechanics Institutes began in Scotland and were the brain-child of Dr. Birkbeck (commemorated in Birkbeck College, London) and first established in 1823. They quickly spread countrywide. The Mechanics Institute in Lewes contained a library and a large lecture hall and charged sixpence per lecture with a subscription of two shillings a quarter. It had 190 members. One of its founders was that John Dudeney, the shepherd schoolmaster, who lived just around the corner in Abinger Place.

It is overlooked by the old Brack Mount which, in 1845, was turned into a pleasure ground owned by the new Lewes Arms, which was re-built in 1825. Continuing over the Castle grounds, the most imposing Castle Gate House, with its huge Doric porch and massive front door, was built in 1830 and, at the foot of Castle Hill, Bartholomew House, an outstanding example of mathematical tiling, was built in 1815. Castle Place was built at the same time.

The Castle itself had fallen on sad times. Its tourney ground was well established as a bowling green, but the structure of the keep and walls was in a poor state after having been much sold off to the townsfolk in 1620 as "Flints at 4d. a load". Leased by the tenant of Barbican House, a wealthy wool-merchant, in 1750, the keep had been converted by him into a summer house which was typical of that age of follies and picturesque ruins.

Fortunately for Lewes, the mid-nineteenth century brought a new awareness of historical research and the value of historic relics. The Sussex Archaeological Society was founded in 1846 and the Castle was leased to it in 1850. In a splendid gesture of generosity, Sir Thomas Stanford bought the Castle property outright for £1,600 in 1922 and gave it to the Society for preservation. With another fine gesture, the Rotary Club of the town have since installed and maintain the floodlighting of the keep on three nights every week.

Anne of Cleves House was similarly bought and presented to the Society by Mr Frank Verrall of Southover in 1923.

Southover had its own elegant Victorian addition in the form of Priory Crescent to add another dimension to the Medieval, Tudor, and Georgian houses of Southover High Street. This was built in 1840. A later crescent of quality housing, in 1870, was the St. Anne's Terrace in Western Road.

Along the latter, and all the other roads leading out of Lewes, trim terraces of small town cottages appeared at this time. All fronted directly onto the street and invariably had the essential iron boot-scraper let into the brickwork at each front door, for old photographs of Victorian street scenes locally give no good impression of either tidiness or cleanliness.

Lansdown Place, along Friars Walk, appeared in 1827, Lansdown Terrace eleven years later, along with town cottages at the end of Southover High Street and, intermittently, on either side of Malling Street and South Street.

Modern development has encroached upon the Downs (the Nevill and Downs Estates and the Wallands) and aligned with the Ouse and the Winterbourne (the Winterbourne and Landport Estates). Beyond the Ouse, Malling has been the recipient of the latest large housing extensions.

A new Magistrates Courts (1986) has been built on the site of the Friars Place and infilling behind here, and in Cliffe etc. has provided added town housing and retirement accommodation. Light industrial works, warehouses and retail enterprises are rapidly covering the area between the Phoenix Causeway and South Malling.

But the most enterprising, by far, of modern development is up the steep slope of Cliffe Hill where Mr Isaac Vinall laid out, or rather hung, his Cuilfail Estate, named after his favourite hill in Scotland. The name bemuses newcomers, perhaps he should have called it "Baldy's Estate"! It is not the most convenient of housing estates. On frozen winter nights cars have to be left at the foot of the hill and the steep lanes climbed on foot, but the view of Lewes and the surrounding countryside is unsurpassed. Moreover it is almost a necessity for any inhabitant of Lewes to be an expert climber. Many of the houses run up hill and down dale as the town itself does, and it is not unusual for every room to have its own personal staircase.

Above Cuilfail, another enterprising developer laid out the airy Lewes Golf Course, reached by way of Chapel Hill, the ancient trackway to the east. Higher than that, failing a space capsule, Lewes cannot go . . . .

XII. LEWES BECOMES A MUNICIPAL BOROUGH

The official boundaries of Lewes eventually swelled to include the spreading population. The old boundary stone outside St. Anne's Church stood as the boundary of the borough until 1881. It still stands but no longer marks the limit of the town for, in 1881, Lewes was made a Municipal Borough and her boundaries were extended to include the Wallands Estate, Southover, Cliffe and South Malling together with the parishes of St. Anne and St. John-sub-Castro. As a Municipal Borough Lewes had at last achieved the status she had long merited.

By the Charter of Incorporation, the last Senior Constable became the first Mayor of the town. He was Alderman Wynne Baxter of the family of John Baxter who established the firm of Baxter and Sons, printers and publishers, on School Hill in 1812.

John Baxter's second son George, an artist and an engraver, invented a process of printing in oil colours and produced prints of rare quality. With his youngest son, John established the Sussex Agricultural Express in 1837 and, in 1824/27, published the, still highly-valued, "History of Sussex" by T. W. Horsfield in two volumes.

Alderman Wynne was a much respected officer in the town, having been High Constable in 1879 and in 1880.

The Town Hall, originally the Star Inn, was rebuilt in its present red brick Victorian style in 1893, although much of the interior is still, fortunately, preserved, including the magnificent Jacobean staircase from Slaugham and much of the old panelling.

As the County Town, new offices have had to be built, and others converted, to accommodate increasing local responsibilities in all walks of life. Following the fine example of the new County Hall, with its Georgian facing of Portland stone built in 1812, a matching extension was added in 1929/30, re-modelling the adjoining former Newcastle House.

County Councils were at last established in place of the overall rule of the Justices of the Peace by the Local Government Act of 1888.

Later, the 19th century County Hall became the Crown Courts, a new County Hall being built behind St. Anne's Crescent. The entrance steps of the former are still the place for public pomp and ceremony at the arrival of the Circuit Judges for the Assize Sessions.

Into the Twentieth Century

As Charter Borough and County Capital, Lewes emerged out of the long Victorian Age to face all the near-catastrophic events and changes of the 20th century. It celebrated the turn of the century with a last act of good sense and philanthropy in the foundation of the Victoria Hospital. This had originally been sited at the foot of School Hill but had quickly outgrown the space available.

By 1910, £7,000 had been gathered, by public subscription, to build the new hospital on its modern site along Nevill Road. The foundation was duly laid by the Duchess of Albany in 1909 and, in February 1910 the completed hospital was opened "In the pouring rain" alas, by H.R.H. Princess Henry of Battenburgh. It stands as a last, and invaluable, monument to the Victorian Age in Lewes.

In addition, a further welcome gift was made to the town just before the century ended. Mr Aubrey Hillman gave the field known as the Dripping Pan, and also the Convent Field and Mount Field adjacent to it, for the perpetual recreation of the town residents in 1895.

Public generosity has, even now, not yet been entirely stifled by the dawning age of Big Business and State Benefits. In 1920, Mr Wynne Baxter gave the town its second most attractive beauty spot, the Pells. He offered it, "In recognition of the kindness he had at all times received from the inhabitants of his native town." How it echoes the words of that other benefactor, Sir Thomas Springett, in long ago Elizabethan Lewes.

In Medieval times, the Pells area is held by some to have been the Swanery of the Prior of St. Pancras. It lies on the edge of the Ouse-Brooks flood land just below the church of St. John-sub-Castro. In 1603, John Rowe, Constable of Lewes, had given to the town that corner of the area which is now the town swimming pool. The adjoining field was opened as a recreation ground in 1897 to celebrate Queen Victoria's Diamond Jubilee.

In 1878, the north arm of the Pells, along Pelham Terrace, was given to the town by Mr Henry Card, High Constable of the Borough. After the final generous gift of Mr Baxter, the complete waterway has now been transformed into an unexpected corner of tranquility, a haven for ducks and other water fowl and a delight for all who enjoy its peace and beauty.

The Pells. Given to the town by Mr Wynne Baxter in 1920, extending the previous gift of Mr Henry Card in 1878. An unexpected corner of beauty and tranquility.

XIII. THE TWENTIETH CENTURY AND THE LAST INVASIONS

The Great Wars that shattered the World of the first half of the 20th century brought surprisingly little outward change to the face of Lewes town. But, by the middle of the century, it was devastatingly clear that the very heart of Lewes was under ferocious attack, not by arrows, cannon or bombing of military siege, but from the traffic of cars, lorries and juggernauts that belched their ear-splitting way up the length of the main street in ever-destructive procession.

To save the town from total wreckage, a by-pass was constructed south of the town across the flat plain of the River Ouse. It diverted all the east to west coastal traffic away from the town with the added bonus that it also gave many people a new and splendid view of the old Priory ruins, with the castle-crowned town as its backcloth.

Perhaps it is as well the holy place does not still stand inhabited by monks, for the noise of the traffic would have sorely shattered the peace of their lives just as the railway had carved into the peace of their dead.

Travelling from Brighton, in the west, one crosses the Ouse and turns north along its banks to enter the town by the most imaginative piece of road planning in the South — The Lewes Tunnel. Named "The Cuilfail Tunnel" after the estate that overlooks it, it leaves South Street untouched and swings into Lewes where the road from eastern Sussex joins it. At the join a somewhat enthusiastic designer raised a monument in the shape of an ammonite. Not to the memory of the geologist Dr. Mantell, but to celebrate the successful mining through the fossil-laden chalk.

Opening day of the tunnel was a great occasion but not nearly so well attended as the previous day when the tunnel had been declared open to the passage of pedestrians for the first, and possibly the last, time in its history. All Sussex arrived to perambulate. Backwards and forwards they walked, on foot, in wheelchairs, in prams and even on roller-skates, all afternoon. The time was extended hour by hour until only the coming of night saw the crowds dwindle and eventually disappear well-satisfied. Lewes had approved of her innovative road tunnel.

To bring the road into the town a new, wide bridge was flung across the Ouse. It was named after the old iron foundry that had stood on the banks of the river here, the Phoenix Causeway. The name has an optimistic ring about it and bodes well for its use long into the future and it has undoubtedly done much to relieve the olde faithful Cliffe Bridge of strain and wear.

Lewes was to suffer yet one further invasion in her long history, this time by storm.

On the night of October 15/16th, 1987, a hurricane hit the south-east coast of England with horrendous force. Lewes, high on her hill, was battered beyond belief. When morning came and the winds began to abate, her streets ran red in the growing light. Not with blood, for it had been a veritable night of miracles as far as human life was concerned, but red with tiles and bricks, chimneys and glass.

Fortunately there was little enough traffic coming into the town since every road in the surrounding county was also blocked by fallen trees and wreckage. The Grange Gardens were a sad sight and the huge trees, down at the Pells, lay like fallen soldiers in martial lines. For month after month following, every other house in the town wore a huge tarpaulin, rather like elderly gentlemen, caught out in the rain shielding their heads with a waterproof.

But Lewes recovered, as did everywhere else. It was just one more in a long line of attacks that has made her what she is today, a tough old lady and as venerable as England is herself.

She is still independent thinking and still close with her treasures for they are a fragile inheritance in this often thoughtless age. Close with her thoughts too and little given to self-advertisement. But proud to be herself. The toast at civic banquets is still, "The County Town". She is stubborn, English born and bred and Sussex to the core.

Come to her when night falls on a Thursday, Friday or Saturday. Then the Castle is lit up from below and floats, like a magic citadel, on a dark sea. And then Lewes is indeed, "A city set on a hill", whose light cannot be hidden. Long may her light shine out, in welcome, courage and kindliness, through the centuries to come.

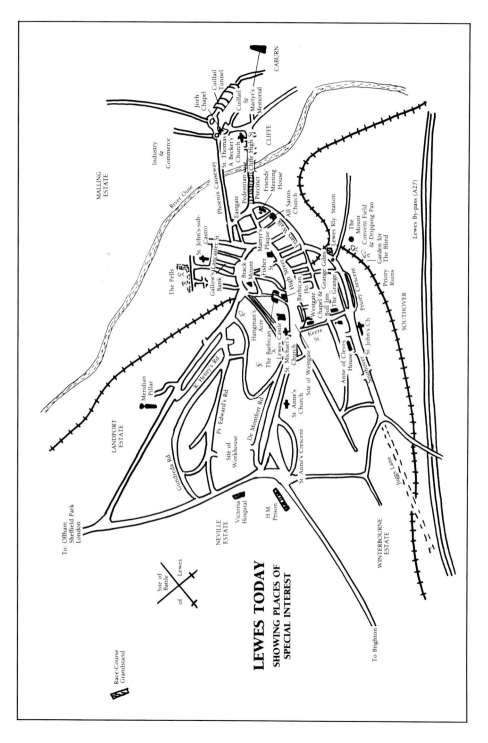

LEWES TODAY

SHOWING PLACES OF SPECIAL INTEREST

Race-Course Grandstand

Site of Battle of Lewes

To: Offham
Sheffield Park
London

NEVILLE
ESTATE

Victoria
Hospital

H.M.
Prison

LANDPORT
ESTATE

Meridian
Pillar

K. Henry's Rd

Gundreda Rd

Pr. Edward's Rd

Site of
Workhouse

De Montfort Rd

St. Anne's Crescent

St. Anne's
Church

MALLING
ESTATE

The Pells

River Ouse

Industry
&
Commerce

St. John's-sub-Castro

Gallows Bank

Lancaster St.

Brack Mount

Hangman's Acre

The Barbican

Lewes Castle

St. Michael's Church

Site of Westgate

Westgate

Keere St.

Anne of Cleves House

Southover

Jireh Chapel

Cuilfail Tunnel

Cuilfail

Phoenix Causeway

St. Thomas A Becket's Church

Cliffe High St.

Martyr's Memorial

CLIFFE

CABURN

Eastgate

Pedestrian Precinct

Friends' Meeting House

All Saints Church

Martyr's Plaque

Mount St.

Fisher St.

High Street

Barbican Ho.

Chapel & Bull Inn.

Grange Gdns

The Grange

St. John's Ch

Priory Crescent

Lewes Rly. Station

The Mount

Convent Field & Dripping Pan

Garden for The Blind

Priory Ruins

SOUTHOVER

Lewes By-pass (A27)

WINTERBOURNE
ESTATE

Juggs Lane

To Brighton

PLACES OF SPECIAL INTEREST

LEWES CASTLE	Open daily 10.00-17.30
MUSEUM OF SUSSEX ARCHAEOLOGY (Barbican House)	Suns. & Bank Hol. 11.00-17.30
LEWES LIVING HISTORY MODEL	Apr./Oct. daily 10.00-17.30 Suns. & Bank Hol. 11.00-17.30
ANNE OF CLEVES HOUSE MUSEUM	Apr./Oct. daily 10.00-17.30 Sun. 14.00-17.30
THE PRIORY RUINS	Easily viewed from outside.
PRIORY GATEWAY	View from Southover High Street.
BRACK MOUNT	View from Castle Bank.
THE BARBICAN	View from Castle Precinct.
THE LEWES BATTLE SITE	Approach from the top of Firle Crescent or by "The Motor Road" off Neville Road (A276) beyond the Neville Estate.

ST. ANNE'S CHURCH & HERMIT CELL
ST. JOHN'S CHURCH, SOUTHOVER & DE WARENNE CHAPEL
ST. MICHAEL'S CHURCH & CHURCHYARD
ST. JOHN-SUB-CASTRO & CHURCHYARD
ST. THOMAS Á BECKET'S CHURCH, CLIFFE

Usually all open during the day.
Suns. for Services

THE WESTGATE CHAPEL	Usually open Tues.-Fri. Mornings & Sun. Services
ST. JAMES' HOSPITAL	Closed. View from the Lower Priory School entrance opposite the Southover Grange
JIREH CHAPEL	Closed for repairs.

The following are always open:

KEERE STREET

JUGGS LANE

THE TOWN TWITTENS

HANGMAN'S ACRE

GALLOWS BANK

THE GARDEN FOR THE BLIND

DRIPPING PAN AND MOUNT

CABURN

THE PELLS

THE MARTYR'S MEMORIAL	Approach via the Cuilfail Estate
SOUTHOVER GRANGE GARDENS	Open during the day.

BIBLIOGRAPHY

Books of General English History
British History by Ramsey Muir
History of England by G.M. Trevelyan
English Social History by G.M. Trevelyan
The Changing Face of History by Ed. Hyams
A History of the Church in England by J. R. Moorman
The Constitutional History of England by F.W. Maitland
Medieval Settlement by P.H. Sawyer
Multiple Estates and Early Settlement by G.R.S. Jones
The South Saxons by P. Brandon
Anglo-Saxon England by David Brown
The Anglo-Saxon Chronicles (trans. Anne Savage)

Books on the History of Sussex
The Victoria History of the County of Sussex vol. 7
The History of Sussex by T.W. Horsfield (2 vols), 1824
History, People and Places in East Sussex by B. White
A History of Sussex by J.R. Armstrong
Sussex by Arthur Mee (The King's England Series)
A Short History of Sussex by John Laverson
Sussex River (3) by E. and M. MacCarthy
Sussex in The Great Civil War and the Interregnum by C.T. Stanford
The Rural Economy of Eastern Sussex (1500-1700) by Colin Brent
The Friars of Sussex 1228-1928 by E.B. Poland
Sussex Martyrs of the Reformation by E. Stoneham
Highways and Byways in Sussex by E. Lucas

Books on the History of Lewes
Lewes Bonfire Night by Jim Etherington
The Town Books of Lewes ed. L.F. Salzman
Lewes. Its Religious History by J.M. Connell 1931
Six More English Towns by Clifton-Taylor 1981
A Day's Ramble in Lewes by Gideon Mantell
The Street Names of Lewes by L.S. Davey 1970
Lewes in Old Picture Postcards by Bob Cairns
Some Lewes Men of Note by George Holman 1927
The Visit of William IV and Queen Adelaide to Lewes, 1830 by Gideon Mantell
A History of Lewes by Walter Godfrey
Travellers to the Town by Ruth Cobb
The Lewes Town Walk (E.S.C.C. publication)
A New Guide to Lewes by W. Heneage Legge 1909
Georgian Lewes by Colin Brent
Victorian Lewes by Colin Brent

Collected Pamphlets on Lewes
The Battle of Lewes 1264 by E. L. Mann
Lewes Castle by Walter Godfrey
Pelham House (County Records Office)
Keere Street by John Houghton
The Priory of St. Pancras by W.H. Godfrey
At the Sign of the Bull by W.H. Godfrey
Some Lewes Towns-folk of the Past by W.H. Godfrey

Guides
History Trail of Lewes by E. & M. McCarthy
Historic Lewes and its Buildings by Colin Brent (Lewes Town Council Official Guide)
Lewes Official Guide by Walter Godfrey
Hamsey Illustrated Guide by R.E.A. Lloyd
Firle Place Illustrated Guide
Sheffield Park Illustrated Guide
Goodwood Illustrated Guide
Rye Illustrated Guide

Most of the above can be found in the Lewes Public Library. The excellent Town Council Official Guide is on sale in the town.

The Museum at Barbican House and the Museum at Anne of Cleve's House, in Southover, both run by the Sussex Archaeological Society, furnish much visual historical information.

The Town Model is also excellent in presenting an over-all picture of the history of the town.

The Friends of Lewes is a Society dedicated to the good and enhancement of the Town.

The Official Town Information Centre now situated on the corner of Fisher Street and the High Street freely provides advice, help and a welcome to all.

The Lewes Priory is supported by the Lewes Priory Trust to "Complete a programme of consolidation work on the upstanding remains".

GLOSSARY

Agger — Ridge marking site of Roman Road
Andredswald — The woodland of the Central Weald (Anglo-Saxon)
Bostal — Ancient trackway
Burg or Burgh — Town
Burghal Hidage — Document of town defence plans based on land tenure
Burgage — Tenure of land in a town
Cottar — Peasant occupying cottage and labouring
Clegg — Coloquial 'sticky clay'
Dene — Wooded valley
Fosse — Ditch alongside Roman road or fortification
Fyrd — Army of Anglo-Saxon militia
Hlaew — Hill or burial ground, Anglo-Saxon
Hurst — Wooded hillock
'ing — Belonging to . . .
Juggs — Panniers
Ley — Land under grass
Lynchet — Low ridge from prehistoric ploughing on a slope
Moot — Assembly
Thegn — One holding land from a superior, a liege-man or thane
Villani — Feudal serf

INDEX